Phil

The Pocket Essential

AMERICAN CIVIL WAR

www.pocketessentials.com

First published in Great Britain 2001 by Pocket Essentials, 18 Coleswood Road, Harpenden, Herts, AL5 1EQ

Distributed in the USA by Trafalgar Square Publishing, PO Box 257, Howe Hill Road, North Pomfret, Vermont 05053

Copyright © Phil Davies 2001
Series Editor: Nick Rennison

The right of Phil Davies to be identified as the author of this work has been asserted by him in accordance with the Copyright, Designs and Patents Act 1988.

All rights reserved. No part of this book may be reproduced, stored in or introduced into a retrieval system, or transmitted, in any form, or by any means (electronic, mechanical, photocopying, recording or otherwise) without the written permission of the publisher.
Any person who does any unauthorised act in relation to this publication may be liable to criminal prosecution and civil claims for damages. The book is sold subject to the condition that it shall not, by way of trade or otherwise, be lent, re-sold, hired out or otherwise circulated, without the publisher's prior consent, in any form or binding or cover other than in which it is published, and without similar conditions, including this condition being imposed on the subsequent publication.

A CIP catalogue record for this book is available from the British Library.

ISBN 1-903047-72-2

2 4 6 8 10 9 7 5 3 1

Book typeset by Pdunk
Printed and bound by Cox & Wyman

Contents

CONTENTS

Part One: The Causes

A House Divided

Secession, Union And The Ideals Of The Republic

Slavery was the cause of the bloodiest war in America's history. But when the conflict began in 1861, both North and South pointedly failed to mention the 'peculiar institution', as slavery was called, in the statement of their war aims. The North fought, it said, in order to maintain the Union, threatened by the rebellion of the eleven seceding states: the South, to protect their freedom from the threat posed by a central government it considered tyrannous. Only gradually did the role of slavery come to be openly acknowledged. In September 1862 Lincoln issued his Emancipation Proclamation, which avowed the aim of freeing the slaves in the Confederacy, and thus made abolition one of the North's central war aims. On one level this was because the Confederacy needed the slaves to keep their armies in the field: to free them was to undermine their effectiveness. Abolition could be seen, then, as a means to an end. But there was another aspect. Slavery made possible a distinct, Southern way of life; it was central to a social system that embodied an interpretation of the legacy of the Founding Fathers, an interpretation not shared by the North. In making abolition an aim, Lincoln acknowledged the true nature of the conflict: it was a war to decide the ascendancy of rival versions of the Republic, of the kind of freedom Republican social and political institutions should promote.

What were these rival views of Republican freedom? For the South, the freedom at issue was chiefly negative. Republican institutions should guarantee the individual freedom from unwarranted interference by religious or secular authorities. How a man lived, what he thought and read, how he disposed of his property – such things should be the concern of the man whose life, thoughts and property they were, and of no one else. This view presumed that the individual was already equipped with the means of leading a fulfilling life: education, property and profession. It was an eighteenth century view of freedom and of the place of government in promoting it. Government was apt to overstep its bounds, and the hallmark of a wise constitution was that it inhibited that tendency as much as possible. For the archetypal Southerner, the big plantation owner, whose lifestyle and aspirations set the pattern even for those Southerners who resented the dominance of the slave-owning aristocracy, the negative freedom that most concerned him was the freedom to dispose of his property as he wished, specifically, the property consisting in other human beings. The Founding Fathers, he insisted, had expressly designed the Constitution to protect such a freedom, and had fought a war because Britain had interfered unjustly with the right to property.

The North, on the other hand, nurtured a richer idea of freedom and of the role of government. First, it must be emphasised that what I have termed the negative view of freedom, was in many ways as important to the North as to the South. The idea of being permitted to get on with making the most of one's life, undisturbed by outside interference, was common currency. But in the North people pursued the goals of happiness and self-fulfilment under conditions that led them to ascribe a positive value to strong central government, one ready to intervene in the citizen's everyday life to a degree obnoxious to a Southerner. The infant factories of the Northeast required the protection and support of Federal financial institutions to stave off foreign competition, until such time as they had become established. The farmers of the Northwest needed government investment in infrastructure to enable their surpluses to reach foreign markets. Moreover, the rapid growth of industries and towns, fuelled by immigration, gave rise to searching questions about the conditions under which meaningful freedom could be exercised. The needs for education, healthcare and housing could not be so effortlessly met in the urban-industrial North as they could be in the South; the traditional and rudimentary institutions that supplied the South's needs were inadequate to those of the fast-growing and sophisticated North. Charitable bodies, religious foundations, local and central government were all involved in helping to provide the necessary conditions for the pursuit of individual fulfilment. The idea that the fruit of freedom – happiness – would fall into one's lap if only one was left alone, gave place to serious reflection on the variety of social and political forces involved in its growth.

The North and South also differed over the place of the Union in securing the freedoms enshrined in the Constitution and the Declaration of Independence. The Southern view was that the original states, the colonies, had formed an alliance, the Union, to make possible a form of social life that gave those freedoms unfettered expression. It had an instrumental value; the Union had no intrinsic worth aside from the freedoms it helped promote. This is not to say that Southerners had no love for it. The Confederacy's premier general, R E Lee, and its president, Jefferson Davis, both bitterly regretted being forced into taking up arms against it. For the North, on the other hand, the idea of the Union had become entwined with the Constitution and the Declaration of Independence; the vision of the Founding Fathers had, they believed, its unique expression in the Federal Union. It was Lincoln who supplied the rationale of this. The Republic represented an experiment in radical democracy – government by, for and of the people. But that experiment would stand refuted if it failed to pass a crucial test: the provision of a stable and enduring form of government. For all its virtues, the Republican ideal would be worthless if it allowed the dissolution of the commonwealth into fragments.

When the South considered the Union a threat to freedoms it had hitherto nurtured, it felt it had no choice but to leave. But for the North, the Union was not essentially about guaranteeing the freedom of property, or any other one specific form of freedom. What was at stake was the preservation of a form of government that fostered the free development of all individuals equally. And this brings us back to the slaves. For, in the North, public conscience grew ever more restive at the fact that a nation, founded on freedom, held in servitude four million of its inhabitants.

Slavery And 'King Cotton'

The establishment of the new republic in 1776 with slavery as a part of its fabric was one of the most important legacies of the Founding Fathers – Jefferson and Washington, Madison, Hamilton and Adams. Slavery was an embarrassment to them; it was not explicitly referred to in the original version of the Constitution. Thomas Jefferson, sole author of that paean to liberty, the Declaration of Independence, was himself a slave owner, albeit an unhappy one. He likened the problem presented by slavery to holding a 'wolf by the ears': 'we can neither hold him, nor safely let him go. Justice is in the one scale, self-preservation in the other.' In the New England states, slavery had ceased to have any economic value, but to the south, in Virginia, Georgia and the Carolinas, slaves in large numbers worked plantations that grew the rice, sugar and, above all, tobacco on which the wealth of Southerners depended. Apart from the economic problem posed by freeing the slaves, there was the vexed question of what to do with them once they were set free. So the Founding Fathers decided to ignore the issue, hoping that time would provide the solution.

That a nation whose defining property was the advocacy of freedom should rest a crucial part of its economy on servile labour was, of course, absurd. Public opinion was aware of this from the outset, and was made increasingly uneasy by it. In the North, this helped feed the movement for abolition. In the South, it bred a defensive outlook, founded on unacknowledged guilt that expressed itself in proslavery apologetics. The tide of international opinion was turning irrevocably against slavery; in 1807, Britain outlawed the slave trade, although it would not abolish slavery itself until the 1830s. In an age of free-market capitalism, servile labour made no economic sense. Sooner or later, Jefferson's generation thought, the South's dependence on the 'peculiar institution' would be made redundant by progress.

But in the decades following independence, instead of declining, the slave-based sector of the American economy enjoyed a boom. There were two causes: Eli Whitney, and the textile revolution in Britain and northern Europe. In the second half of the eighteenth century, the application of new technologies to the production of textiles created a huge demand for cotton. At first this was of no benefit to the South. Though it could grow cotton in abundance, it could not profitably turn this into lint (the form in which cotton was delivered to the factories). It took one slave a whole day to remove the seeds from enough cotton to produce one pound of lint. But in 1793 Eli Whitney, on a visit to a friend's plantation, came up with a solution. He devised an 'engine' to separate the seeds from the cotton fibres; Whitney's 'Gin' enabled one slave to produce a thousand pounds of lint per day. Cotton exports to Europe soared, and with them the demand for slaves.

By 1860 one in three persons in the Southern States belonged to another; in a population of twelve million, four were slaves. The cotton belt formed a crescent that stretched from Virginia southwest through the Deep South – Alabama, Mississippi, Louisiana and Texas – and northwest into Arkansas, across the Mississippi River. Three quarters of the cotton used by European mills came from this region. Southern planters made fortunes, and built elaborate Palladian-style mansions, reinvesting their profits in the purchase of additional land and slaves wherever possible. European demand for Southern cotton seemed inexhaustible, and fostered in the South an exaggerated assessment of the support it could command in Britain and France. 'Cotton is King,' declared James Hammond in a famous speech before the Senate. When war broke out, Southerners were confident that British dependence on their cotton would force intervention on their behalf. In 1861, one South Carolinian told a British visitor that he expected Her Majesty's fleet, sooner or later, to come and destroy the Yankee ships that were blockading Southern harbours, choking off the supply of cotton.

At home also the South was inclined to overemphasise its place on the domestic scene. It considered its contribution to the nation's economy was poorly recompensed and seldom adequately acknowledged. All but a quarter of the country's exports consisted of cotton. Badly needed foreign exchange was generated largely by the activity of slave-owners. The economy was growing, thanks chiefly to King Cotton, and the treasury was feeling the benefit but Southerners felt they were unfairly treated. The Northwest received ample assistance from the government to develop its roads, waterways and rail links, employing money indirectly created by Southerners, while the fledgling industries of the Northeast were assisted by import duties they considered iniquitous. To enable domestic manufactures to find their feet, Southerners were expected to pay artificially inflated prices for goods imported from abroad.

But the loud and bruising self-confidence of Southerners was, in part, the outcome of deep-seated anxieties. They lived in constant fear of slave insurrections. In large tracts of the country, blacks were in the majority; in Virginia the ratio was three to one. In 1822 the slave Denmark Vesey led an abortive revolt. Ten years later, in the insurrection led by Nat Turner, sixty Virginians were murdered. Fearing that the very possibility of freedom could be an incitement to revolt, some states outlawed emancipation. Liberal-minded slave-owners felt compelled to defer emancipating their slaves, fearful of the possible impact among slaves whose masters were less liberally inclined.

In an effort to address their fear and guilt, Southerners engaged in a spurious defence of the 'peculiar institution'. They insisted on its alleged social and moral benefits. It was the only viable basis of true democracy. Freed from the degradation of manual toil, whites could engage in the higher issues of communal life, science and the arts. They pointed out that the model of the democratic form of government, ancient Athens, had itself been carried on the backs of slaves. Besides, the black man was fitted by temperament for such bondage; his childishness, lack of industry and complete fecklessness rendered him a permanent child. The planter stood to his slaves as a father to his children; and indeed, one of the great abuses of the system was that so many of the mulatto children on an estate bore a striking resemblance to their master's legitimate progeny.

The appeal of such nonsense may appear less bizarre if one bears in mind the lack of a comprehensive and coherent alternative. On the eve of war it was estimated that two billion dollars was invested in 'slave property'; the whole Southern social and economic structure was implicated. Given the choice between complete ruin and persistence in gross, but

11

inherited, injustice, it is difficult not to sympathise with the choice most Southerners made.

The majority of white Southerners did not own slaves. Of eight million whites in the South only 400,000 owned ten or more slaves, the number needed for a plantation. Southern society was fraught with tensions arising from the conflict between the planter aristocracy and so-called 'poor whites'. The plantations tended to occupy the lower and more fertile lands along the coastal plains and the river valleys of the Deep South. Up-country districts, like the mountainous regions of eastern Tennessee, northern Georgia and western Virginia were home to small farmsteads, producing hogs, corn and whiskey for local markets, without the aid of slave labour. In such areas, whites either detested the 'peculiar institution' or at most owned one or two slaves. Their dislike was as much for the Negro as his state of bondage. But though hostile to the planter class who controlled state and county politics, they would rally to its support against Yankee criticism. 'Poor whites' felt they had a stake in the social system whose key component was slave labour. A social system in which the hated Negro was given an unalterable place at the bottom of the ladder reassured them of their intrinsic worth, based on skin colour alone, and protected them from the awful prospect of competing for land and employment with millions of ex-slaves.

The Character Of The North

Regional self-consciousness grew apace in the decades before the war. North and South came to view each other as the advocates of incompatible ideals. Public debate was conducted in a distorting rhetoric that inhibited rational discussion, promoting, instead, a conviction of irreconcilable antagonism. 'North and South,' wrote Savannah lawyer and planter, Charles B. Jones, ' have been so entirely separated by climate, by morals, by religion, and by estimates so entirely opposite of all that constitutes honour, truth and manliness, that they cannot longer exist under the same government.' We have seen something of the forces underpinning the distinctive character of the South. It is time to take a look at the North.

Marx thought of the war as a struggle between the South's feudal landed gentry and the North's urban-industrial elite, the vanguard of capitalism in its early stages. Though crude, there is some truth in this view. In the North there was a substantial shift of population towards the towns. Between 1800 and 1860 the agricultural labourers dropped from 70% to 40% of the work force; in the South it stayed at 80%. Of Southerners one in ten lived in towns, of Northerners one in four. None the less it should be pointed out that the vast majority of towns had no more than a few thousand inhabitants. The giant cities, like New York, Cincinnati and Chicago, with scores of thousands, were the exception, looked on with awe by Southerners and Northerners alike. In Pennsylvania, New York State and elsewhere in the Northeast, the manufacture of cloth, clothing, footwear, iron and steel had displaced in importance the agriculture that had formerly dominated the region. Wage-labour, the Southerner claimed, was inimical to the ideals of the Republic. It bred a culture of dependency; the 'wage-slaves' of the factories led miserable lives, paid no more than necessary to keep body and soul together, faced with the prospect of being thrown out of work at the next slump. Under such conditions, men became meanly obsessed with their own narrowly conceived self-interests, ready to dispose of their votes as powerful demagogues or the bosses dictated. The spread of factories meant the inexorable destruction of virtues requisite for the responsible exercise of citizenship – a view found both in the North as well as the South.

Further west, north of the Ohio River the main source of income was still chiefly farming. Cereal crops were grown for export to markets in the east and, thence, across to Europe. The 'Old Northwest', as the region was known, was home to two distinct groups. The first wave settlers to the region had come from Virginia and the Carolinas, fleeing the dominance of the planter aristocracy, and they gave to the southern portion of the Northwest, where they settled, its distinctive character. To the north, settlers from the Northeast had taken possession. On a reduced scale, the enmity between the Yankee and Southern halves of the Northwest mirrored that of the North and South. But the two found in the bound of common interests a force stronger than atavistic hatred. Movement of crops and livestock to market required the building of railroads, canals and turnpikes. They looked to the Federal government to pay for these. This brought them, Yankees and former Southerners alike, into conflict with the South, which, as we have seen, resented the wealth they thought they had created being spent for the benefit of a region other than their own.

Another important factor in the North's distinctive make-up was immigration. In the 1840s and 1850s political unrest and famine in Europe forced over three million people, principally Irish and Germans, to seek refuge in the States. They settled in the towns of the Northeast that were the centres of manufacturing and distribution, or took to farming in the Northwest. Few settled in the South where the dominant position of the slave economy left few opportunities for people who had nothing but their labour to sell. The vast majority of these people were Catholic. The first settlers, and their descendants had been Protestants. Distrust of Catholicism was part of their legacy to the citizens of the new republic. The arrival of large numbers of Catholics caused considerable unrest in the North, and lead to the formation of a powerful anti-immigrant, anti-Catholic political party. Eventually, 'Nativist' agitation died down. But to the average Southerner it enhanced his belief in the fundamental otherness of the North.

Abolition Movement

The plight of the Negro generated a mixed response in the North. Hostility to the 'peculiar institution' was targeted more on the unfair economic and political advantages it conferred on the South's planter aristocracy, than its morally obnoxious character. Nevertheless, there was widespread recognition that the existence of slavery constituted a contradiction at the heart of a government whose founding documents, continually and self-consciously cited in political disputes at all levels of society, championed freedom in all its forms. Moderate opinion in the North viewed the elimination of slavery as a long term goal – Lincoln in the 1840s thought that it might disappear by the end of the century – but decided that the best approach was a policy of containment; leave it alone where it currently existed, and try to ensure that it did not spread west to the new territories. As it turned out, it was the relentless expansion westward that was to turn slavery and its fate into a national stumbling block. Meanwhile, the prevalence of abolitionist sentiment ensured that all discussions about the 'peculiar institution' were conducted in an atmosphere of rancour and intolerance. The campaign conducted by abolitionists caused the South to rally round the cause of the 'peculiar institution', and to reject out of hand even the most modest proposal for its termination. Abolitionism helped make it impossible for Northerners and Southerners to address the common problems of how to deal with the economic dislocation resulting from abolition, and of what to do with four million former slaves.

The abolition movement was part and parcel of what is known as the Second Great Awakening, a popular movement for moral reform in all sections of society, whose scope ranged from temperance, to votes for women, from vegetarianism to emancipation of the slaves. The leading figure of the movement was William Lloyd Garrison, whose paper, *The Liberator*, was a redoubtable vehicle for the dissemination of abolitionist propaganda. Hostile to organised government, he preferred to address individuals directly through speeches and leaflets, millions of which bombarded all regions of the South in the 1840s and 1850s. The single biggest block of support came, unsurprisingly, from the three hundred thousand free blacks living in the North. Their leading light, Stephen Douglass wrote a best-selling autobiography, which had an enormous influence on public opinion in Britain and France. Perhaps the most famous figure in the movement was Harriet Beecher Stowe. *Uncle Tom's Cabin*, published in 1852, sold three million copies in its first year; Queen Victoria wept over it. Lincoln is alleged to have said, on meeting Stowe in 1862, that he was pleased to meet the little lady who had started a great war. It was the depiction of family relations under slavery that, more than anything, roused Northern popular opinion to ire – especially among women. Children separated from their parents, evil masters lusting over their female slaves, a callous disregard for the sanctity of family life – all are major features of the book.

Abolitionists did rouse the conscience of at least a section of the populace. But for most people abolitionist rhetoric offered a powerful means to vent hostility derived, not from moral outrage, but from resentment at the South's economic and political power (in the pre-war years the vast majority of presidents were from south of the Mason-Dixon line). Hatred of slavery, whatever its motivation, was widespread - just as widespread was distaste for its victims. Racism was prevalent among Northerners and Southerners alike. Even among many genuine abolitionists there was a great reluctance to accord the black man equal standing with the white. Men in both North and South alike feared the consequences of a job market in which they would have to compete with liberated slaves. A popular approach to the problem – one endorsed by Lincoln until the eve of the war – was a programme of repatriation. Under it, five thousand slaves were bought free and shipped off to West Africa in the 1850s.

The political expression of anti-slavery sentiment was the Republican Party, formed out of a coalition of groups in the 1850s, and with a moderate platform; its extreme abolitionist wing was not representative of its outlook. Their goal was to contain it within its current limits – the fifteen states whose constitutions permitted slavery. Despite the evidence of the previous half century, they still hoped, as the Founding Fathers had three generations earlier, that changing social and economic conditions would promote its withering away within those limits. Even as late as 1860, in his inaugural speech, Lincoln was reassuring the South that his administration would not attack slavery in those states where it already existed.

15

But for Southerners the mere existence of a party whose platform was its hostility to slavery was a provocation. It was the election of Lincoln, dubbed 'the Black Republican' that triggered the secession of the Southern states in winter 1860-61.

Westward Expansion

A key feature of the Republic's self-image was as the bearer of a divinely ordained task. Its success as a form of government was to prove the validity of government by the people, of the people, and for the people. It was to be an example to the world, and through its agency democracy was to spread to all nations. The duty to expand westwards was an extension of this idea, and known as the doctrine of Manifest Destiny. To vindicate the claim about the divine sanction for their Republic, Americans needed the evidence of success; this was in accord with the deeply ingrained Calvinist idea that divine election to salvation could only be known through the fruits of a man's life. The prosperity that would flow from occupation of the vast lands to the west would serve as material proof of the rightness of the American way. Whether one considers it a cynical cover for imperial ambition, or the expression of sublime collective egoism, the fact remains that Manifest Destiny was enormously influential.

In 1803 Jefferson purchased from Napoleon a vast tract of land (north of Mexico, south of Canada, and west of the Mississippi), known as the Louisiana territory. He expected the rate at which it was settled to be slow: possibly a thousand years. But population expanded at a pace that outstripped all expectations, and lands west of the Mississippi were soon being used to raise crops and cattle. Northerners and Southerners began a struggle for control of the trans-Mississippi area. Issues surrounding the process of expansion provided a focus for tensions between North and South, sharpening the antagonism to the point of belligerency.

Between 1800 and 1850 the population of the Republic quadrupled. On average, a new state entered the union every three years between 1803 and the year war broke out, 1861. With each new territory formed, or state admitted, the question was asked, 'Was it to be slave or free?' On the answer to that question depended the future of the nation. For the South, 'no' meant eventual extinction, for their only hope of survival lay in growth. Each state entering the Union that was not slave would tip the balance of power in Congress still further against the South. For the North, expansion was vital to relieve the pressures and tensions building

16

up as a result of population growth, partly because of immigration. But slave labour, they insisted, could not work side by side with free; aside from the ideological objections, it made no economic sense. The small independent farmer with his hired labour could not possibly compete with a slave-owner. Besides, the abiding aim of the moderate Northern majority was to stifle slavery where it already existed through denying it the opportunity to grow.

But could the lands to the west support a slave-based economy? It is often suggested that the South's struggle for the right to take slaves west was pointless; the region was simply not suitable for plantations. Future states would enter as free, not because of Northern pressure, but because climate and soil dictated it. But what some Southerners were attempting was to keep the door open for their colonisation of still greater regions in the future. Their eyes were focused on Central America, which they hoped to turn into a system of slave states, dominated by Southern interests. Spain's empire in the New World was collapsing. Mexico became an independent republic in 1822, and suffered chronic instability ever after, ceding vast tracts of land to the United States as a result of the war of 1846-48. The whole of Central America was a tangle of impoverished, strife-torn petty states. Spain still held Cuba, but appeared willing to consider selling it; the United States' government was, as late as 1860, trying to negotiate its purchase. Southern adventurers attempted twice to take her by force; in Nicaragua, Southern business and political interests exerted a preponderant influence, until a military coup threw them out. These regions had a history of slave usage; cotton could be grown here, as well as sugar and rice, while the mines were ideal locations for the use of slaves. The idea of a slave empire stretching far south of the Gulf of Florida, though not universally endorsed, was far from being the preserve of a lunatic fringe.

The Road To Sumter, 1820-1861

From The Missouri To The 1850 Compromise

Tensions between North and South first came to a head in 1820, when Missouri sought admission to the Union as a state. Would it enter as a slave or free state? A settlement was agreed, known as the 'Missouri Compromise' that struck a balance between the interests of North and South. It set a precedent that was to ward off crises for the next twenty-five years. Missouri was admitted as a slave state; the additional political representation this gave the South was offset by the admission of Maine, a free state, at the same time. And a dividing line at 36 degrees 30 minutes was drawn westwards to the Pacific, all territory northwards to be free, all southwards slave. This question about political representation merits a moment's comment.

The responsibility for the Louisiana Purchase territories lay in the hands of the Federal government. When areas became sufficiently populous they were eligible for organisation into a legal unit known as a 'territory'; it was from this that states emerged. Up to the level of state, all decisions, including those concerning slavery, were in the hands of the Federal government. Were the controlling majorities in the Senate and the House of Representatives (the two component elements in the Legislature, or, Congress) in the hands of states hostile to slavery, the 'peculiar institution' could be kept from growing. Only by maximising their chances of representation in those two chambers, through the establishment of slave states, could Southerners keep open the prospect of limitless expansion. The larger the number of free states, the weaker the voice of the slave interest in the House of Representatives and the Senate.

The stability that the Missouri Compromise achieved was shattered by the effects of the war with Mexico. In 1846, hoping to annexe Texas (nominally a part of Mexico), California and the vast regions that later became New Mexico and Arizona, the Americans invaded their southern neighbour, ostensibly to assist their former compatriots in Texas. Against colossal odds, they won ten major battles, and entered Mexico City in September 1847. When the peace treaty ceded territory that expanded the Republic by a quarter, the struggle between North and South over the status of the states that would in time emerge from this region erupted again.

After three years of uncertainty and bitter debate, another compromise solution was adopted, one that this time left both sides nurturing a sense of profound dissatisfaction. The 1850 Compromise offered the North

California as a free state, and outlawed the buying and selling of slaves in the District of Columbia (location of the nation's capital, Washington). Against this, it offered the South the admission of Texas with slavery and enacted a Fugitive Slave Law to assist slave-owners in the recovery of runaways. This law especially offended Northern public opinion, as its provisions appeared to violate elementary civil rights. But it was the Compromise's stance on slavery in the rest of the newly acquired region that sowed the seeds of future discord. Declaring that the people of each territory should decide the issue themselves when the time came for them to seek admission to the Union, it effectively abolished the Missouri Compromise line, which had hitherto managed to contain the conflict between North and South. It transferred control over the issue away from Federal government, and into the hands of the local populace – a move that was at the time lauded as a triumph of popular sovereignty, but was in fact an invitation to anarchy. Congress, the traditional forum for deliberating issues of national import, and for framing policies on the basis of national consensus, was declared incompetent to deal with the slavery question. In future, when a territory came to the moment of decision, diehards on both sides would attempt to flood the nascent state with their supporters, hoping to create an electoral majority favourable to their cause. Debate in the national forum was to be replaced by rigged ballots, bribery and intimidation of voters, mob law and murder.

'Bleeding Kansas' And The Dred Scott Case

In 1854 the territory of Kansas asked to join the Union. A neighbouring territory, Nebraska, did the same. It was hoped that the admission of the two states simultaneously would happen without any friction, because it was expected that one would be slave the other free. Following the precedent set by the 1850 Compromise, the decision was referred to the people in the territories concerned. But, whereas neither side thought it worthwhile contesting the status of Nebraska, they fought bitterly over the more southerly Kansas, which shared a border with the slave state of Missouri. Thousands of pro-slave Missourians flocked across the border. Settlers from free states also poured in, eventually outnumbering the pro-slavers. But the Missourians did not intend to submit to the will of the majority. Violent conflict tore the country apart, and a spate of killings on an unprecedented scale swept through Kansas. Through rigged elections, the men from Missouri at first got their way - the territorial legislature voted for slavery. The free majority refused to give way to corruption.

Soon the territory had two legislatures and two constitutions, one slave, one free. Then a horde of pro-slavery men descended on the town of Lawrence, headquarters of anti-slavery, and sacked it, butchering scores of citizens. In retaliation, a fanatical abolitionist, John Brown, who had failed twenty times in business in six states and defaulted on his debts each time, kidnapped five slavers. He and his sons, in cold blood, hacked them to death with broadswords. The fighting that erupted in 1856 was not to end until the close of the Civil War in 1865.

One of the products of the 1850 Compromise was a new political party: the Republicans. Appalled at what were considered outrageous concessions to slavery, various groups from across the North united on a moderate anti-slavery platform. The emergence of a national party, drawing its identity from an anti-Southern programme, further widened the gulf between North and South. Hitherto, political parties had combined within their ranks men from both sections, and this had mitigated the divisive effects of the slavery question. The Dred Scott Decision of 1857 boosted the popularity of the Republicans and drove home the wedge dividing North from South.

The case concerned a slave who sued for freedom on the grounds of prolonged residence in a free state. It came before the Supreme Court, a majority of whose judges were Southern. The claim was dismissed. In his ruling, Chief Justice Taney undercut the basis of Scott's claim. Scott could not claim freedom on the basis of residence in a free area, because the grounds for so designating the area were unsound. A pronouncement of Congress had declared it free, but Congress did not, under the Constitution, have jurisdiction over slavery. The Constitution, he argued, guaranteed the right of property, including property in slaves. It followed that Congress could not legally set limits on where a slaveholder might take his property. Although he did not spell out the, absurd, logic of his argument, others did. If the right to property was so inviolable, then not even a state had the right to outlaw slavery; the free states faced the possibility of their anti-slave legislation being declared unconstitutional. Northerners raged at the Supreme Court being made into the instrument of King Cotton.

John Brown And The Election Of Lincoln

In October 1859, Brown, his sons and a small band of followers seized the Federal arsenal at Harper's Ferry in Virginia. Their aim was to foment a slave rebellion. Captured after a thirty-hour siege by troops under the command of Robert E Lee, Brown was tried and executed in December. Reaction in the North was mixed. Thoreau thought no man ever more justly hanged; Emerson compared him to Christ. A group of respectable abolitionists had funded the raid. When this was discovered Southern opinion went wild. The only Northern comments that registered with them were those favourable to Brown; they demanded a positive demonstration on the part of Northern moderates that they disapproved of Brown's action. Southern Democratic Senators framed a bill, a slave code designed to protect what they claimed were the legitimate rights of property (in slaves). Endorsement of this measure, an outrage to the majority of Northerners, became the only acceptable indication that the North did not secretly gloat over the prospect of a slave insurrection.

The election of Lincoln, the leader of the 'Black Republicans', was the last straw for the South. Almost the moment the election results were announced, Southern secessionists set to work. In December 1860, South Carolina broke away from the Union. In the months that followed, all the states of the Deep South - Georgia, Alabama, Louisiana, Mississippi, Texas, Arkansas, and Florida - followed. In controversies in earlier years, Southern Senators had frequently threatened secession. Particularly in the previous ten years. Men of both sections had come to regard such threats as mere bluster. When secession actually happened, there was a general sense of shock in the North, and a mixture of euphoria and disbelief throughout the South. No one could agree on whether the constitution permitted secession or not. Some claimed that the Union and the States came into existence at the same time, and thus the right of a state to withdraw could not be argued on the basis of a superior authority flowing from its existing prior to the Union. Others said that it was absurd for a government to allow for the possibility of its dissolution. Southerners were adamant that states' rights included the right to secession. On both sides of the Mason-Dixon line, no one was sure what the Federal government had a right to do in this situation. For a range of different reasons, including the alleged pusillanimous character of the Northern male, there was a widespread belief in the South that secession would not lead to war. There were many variations on the claim that all the blood spilt as a consequence of secession would be containable in a thimble.

For a time, it looked like that might be true. In the winter of 1860, a rump of Southern states had withdrawn, but their prospects for long-term survival outside the Union did not look good – unless, that is, some of the upper Southern states joined them. These – such as Virginia and Tennessee – contained what little manufacturing capacity the South possessed; in addition, a considerable percentage of the nation's railroads ran through these areas. In peace or in war, these states would be necessary for the formation of a viable Southern Republic. In full awareness of this, Lincoln's administration played a waiting game.

While the eight renegade states formed a government in Montgomery, Alabama, Lincoln reassured both North and South that he would not be the first to take aggressive action. He declared his intention to fulfil his constitutional duty to uphold such laws as would guarantee the basic freedoms, including freedom to own property. He chose his words and actions carefully, doing all he could to put heart into the moderates and pro-Union men, who he hoped lay temporarily silent in the South. His covert message was: 'I am not about to launch an attack on the 'peculiar institution.' By pursuing the line of least resistance, he hoped to prevent a stampede of the upper Southern states into the arms of the Confederacy. Once the heat of the secessionist moment had cooled, moderates in the South might coax the rebel states back into the Union.

Instead, the bombardment of Fort Sumter in April 1861 plunged the country into war.

Set in the harbour of Charleston, the very heart of secessionist agitation, it could not long remain in the hands of Federal authorities without being challenged. The tiny Union force holding Sumter was regarded by the newly independent South Carolina as an affront to its sovereignty. Although both Jefferson Davis, the South's newly elected president, and Lincoln played for time, local patriots were determined to force the issue. The governor of the state had been quick to mobilise his militia, putting him in possession of the largest body of troops currently in existence in the South. General Beauregard, commander of the state militia, ordered his batteries to open fire at 4.30 on the morning of 12 April.

Part Two: The Opponents

Armies, Population And Industry

The Army Before The War

The standing army numbered fewer than 17,000 officers and men, most of them spread along the western frontier. Only two officers had ever commanded more than a brigade in combat. The commander in chief was Lieutenant General Winfield Scott, a veteran of the Mexican War of the 1840s in which he had distinguished himself, winning numerous battles against superior numbers. Now past seventy, dropsical and overweight, he was unable to mount a horse and frequently napped in staff meetings. There was no general staff, no plan of mobilisation, and few detailed and reliable maps; when Union General Halleck was planning his campaign in the West, he had to buy his maps from a bookshop in Memphis. West Point, the nation's premier military academy, devoted more attention to the science of fortification, engineering and mathematics than it did to strategy or battlefield tactics. Its teaching of tactics was outmoded, derived from the study of Napoleon's campaigns, fought half a century earlier. The chief lesson they learnt from this, and from the experience of the Mexican War and the War of 1812, was the importance of attack. The tactical offensive, however, suited to troops armed with smoothbore muskets was inappropriate in the age of the rifle. The Civil War infantryman carried a Springfield or British-made Enfield rifle, with an effective range of 750 yards; smoothbores were limited to around 75. The extremely high casualty rates in the war (30% was not uncommon) were due to officers being slow to react to the implications of the new technology, persisting in close order attacks against troops armed with rifles and firing from entrenched positions.

Training for the rank and file was rudimentary: basic arms drill, plenty of marching and getting into line formation from column and back again, with a bit of practice in skirmishing (the widely spaced, loose order line that preceded the main force in battle). But there was little target practice and no mock battles. Even the column and line formation drill was of limited use, as the units involved were rarely bigger than companies. In the coming war, on the other hand, troops were going to be deployed in far larger numbers. The success of attacks undertaken by massed troops would depend on effective co-ordination, which they would have to learn on the job, paying a high price in dead and wounded while they did so.

In addition to the regular army, there were the state militias – volunteer regiments composed of companies raised from towns and counties, consisting of men who played soldier in their spare time. These rarely met in regimental strength, and then only for parades and grand reviews; a member of a militia unit was as likely to spend his time in band practice as in arms drill. Yet it was from this source that the four million who served on both sides were drawn. The Federal and Confederate governments relied mostly on the machinery of the separate states, that is, on the state militias, to raise their volunteer armies.

Volunteer Troops And Their Leaders

It is often said that Confederate had the advantage over Union troops because of their natural ability as fighters. Southern pluck and dash, derived from mythical Cavalier ancestry, meant that rebel armies, and especially the cavalry, repeatedly outfought the pasty city boys, many of them Irish or German immigrants, who filled the ranks of the Union. At the outset of the war, it was widely believed in the South that one rebel would be a match for ten of the enemy. And indeed, the combat record of the first two years does something to bear this out.

Seven of the nation's eight military academies were in the South; among the Southern gentry a far higher proportion pursued a military career than their Northern equivalents. The percentage of the population living in towns was far smaller in the South, and consequently the pursuit of rural sports, involving guns and horses, far more common. Until 1863, the Union was unable to match the cavalry units commanded by such men as J E B Stuart and Nathan Bedford Forrest. Southerners supplied their own mounts, and exhibited a zeal for freestyle fighting that outclassed Union cavalrymen, at least in the first half of the war. Rebel cavalry tended to operate in force and independently of the infantry, while the Union troopers found themselves broken up into smaller units and assigned duties of a less glamorous kind. While rebel cavalry exulted in daring sorties deep behind enemy lines, its counterpart was restricted to guarding baggage trains, which stifled its esprit de corps and will to fight.

But in time, as a result of the lessons of bitter experience in combat, Union troopers were able to steal some of the rebel horsemen's thunder.

If Southern cavalry were generally superior to that of the North, the same is certainly not true of their infantry. The first major clash of the war, Bull Run, proved that Billy Yank could fight with as much determination and skill as Johnny Reb. But rebel infantry were, initially, better led. From second lieutenants up to major generals, the South had a clear advantage in the quality of its leadership. Two thirds of the pre-war officer corps chose to fight for the Confederacy, among them some of the greatest names in the conflict – Robert E. Lee and Thomas J. Jackson, for example. Starting its army from scratch, the Confederacy spread its leadership and military expertise evenly throughout its newly formed units. The officers and men who stayed loyal to the Union, on the other hand, were not put to such good use. The head of the Union forces, General Scott, decided not to disperse his regular officers and NCOs among the fast growing volunteer force, but to keep them separate in their already existing units. Regiments of volunteers, commanded by volunteers, paid a terrible price for their lack of knowledge. Without the guidance of experienced soldiers, volunteer units were left to make all kinds of elementary errors on the battlefield.

Both sides, however, suffered the mixed blessing of elected officers and 'political' generals. Used to voting for everything from the county sheriff to the state governor, volunteers, both Union and Confederate, saw no reason why they should not elect their officers too. Through four years of fighting, the democratic spirit never really gave way to the martinet automatism of a professional army. (The Prussian general, Von Moltke, famously described the men who fought the war as 'armed mobs'.) To begin with, units were inclined to debate the wisdom of orders rather than carry them out unquestioningly. Given the enormous scale of the armies, and the paucity of trained military personnel, the system of election was possibly no worse a way of picking leaders than any other – at any rate, the trial and error of actual combat soon showed who was hopelessly unfit to lead, while providing on-the-job training for the remainder. The efficacy of 'political' generals is similarly ambivalent. The vote-winning value of military command was enormous. Both Democrats and Republicans tried to get reliable party members - possible future candidates for high office - appointed as generals. General Fremont, Republican presidential candidate in the 1856 election, who bungled his way through campaigns in Missouri and West Virginia before being retired out of the army, is a good example of how much harm this system could cause. At the same time, plenty of professionally trained soldiers who became generals did no better. As with elected officers, what really mattered was not the provenance of the appointment, so much as how they responded to the demands of the job.

Population, Manufacturing And Wealth

'God,' said Napoleon, 'is on the side of the big battalions.' The South may have started with an advantage in the quality of its armies, but it was no match for the North's economic strength – its material wealth, industrial capacity and vast population.

How did the two sides compare in terms of population? There were eighteen million in the states that chose to stay with the Union, as opposed to twelve million in those that opted for secession, and a third of those were slaves. The consequent disparity in the numbers available for combat was not quite as large as these figures suggest. Many of the North's population were unavailable to fight simply because they lived too far away, in California or Oregon Territory. In addition, many of those in the border states of Maryland, Missouri and Kentucky, officially loyal to the Union, fought for the South. The 'peculiar institution' reduced the odds in favour of the North still further: where the wheat of Ohio had to be harvested by men who would otherwise be bearing arms, the sweet potatoes of Georgia were gathered by slaves. Indeed, for the first year or so of the war, the Confederacy was just about able to match the numbers the Union managed to arm and train. This was because the South got a head start in mobilising their forces. The seven states that seceded during the winter of 1860-1 began recruiting and arming their militias at once, seizing the Federal arsenals scattered throughout their regions. Despite these factors, the North possessed a clear superiority in manpower. By the end of the war, it had armed nearly three million men to the Confederacy's million and a quarter.

In manufacturing capacity the South was hopelessly outclassed. The North had 90% of the nation's factories: 97% of its firearms, 94% of its textiles, 93% of its pig iron, and 90% of its footwear. Though it had for years grown the cotton from which the nation's clothing was woven, the South had never bothered to develop its own textile industry. In a matter of months, rebel armies were to acquire the ragged, ill-shod appearance that was to be as much their hallmark as the famous rebel yell, their bloodcurdling battle cry. They came to rely on Federal supply dumps for their shoes and boots, and other necessities, carrying out daring raids and plundering what their own factories were unable to supply. What little clothing the Confederacy managed to produce was, quite literally, home-spun - produced by the wives and mothers of Confederate soldiers. Grey dye was in short supply. They improvised, but couldn't get the colour right; the resulting butternut colour was almost as common in the ranks as the grey officially adopted by the army.

There were only two ironworks in the South: Richmond, Virginia, and Clarksville, Tennessee, the latter of which was lost to Federal invasion within the first year. Coal, copper, iron and precious metals, found in abundance in the North, were virtually non-existent in the South. West Virginia, an area rich in coal, refused to follow the rest of the state when the legislature of Virginia voted to secede; instead it became a new, pro-Union state in its own right. Railroads, canal systems and macadamised roads - common features of Northern topography - were scarce in the South. Lacking the expertise and the heavy industrial plant required, Southern rolling stock and rails deteriorated to the point of collapse; when locomotives broke down they stayed defunct, when Northern cavalry tore up railroad track the lines stayed out of commission. The war was fought over vast stretches of territory, and an efficient, well-kept railroad would have allowed the Southern armies to concentrate rapidly and in strength where needed, helping to offset the numerical superiority enjoyed, particularly later in the war, by its opponent.

If there was some truth to the popular image of Confederates as suave and dashing 'Cavaliers', there was also something to the Southerner's view, usually expressed with a sneer, that the North was a 'nation' of clerks and shopkeepers. A much higher proportion of the population was engaged in commercial and administrative functions in the North than in the South; and this proved greatly to the former's advantage. The management skills bred by a culture of commerce were invaluable to the Northern war effort; they made it possible to raise vast armies to invade and occupy a country the size of European Russia. Where the rebel armies, being on their home territory, could rely sources of supply nearer to hand, an invading Union army had to carry with it the means for creating and protecting a line of supply in a country swarming with enemy partisan groups. Typically, an army of 100,000 required 2,500 wagons, 35,000 draught animals and 600 tons of fodder a day. When McClellan took the Army of the Potomac south to the Yorktown Peninsular in the spring of 1862, he had 115,000 combatants with him. The North could not only equip such a force, but could also meet the logistical challenge of sending it over two hundred miles across water and preparing it for a siege of the Southern capital, Richmond.

Despite its lack of resources and limited managerial expertise, however, the Confederacy worked miracles in producing weapons. This was due largely to the head of its Ordnance Bureau, Josiah Gorgas. To begin with, the South had only one factory for producing artillery (the Tredegar Ironworks in Richmond), and only the looted machinery from the Federal arsenal at Harpers Ferry for manufacturing rifles. But it had no nitre, the main component in gunpowder. Munitions factories were set up all over the South. Gorgas persuaded the women of the Confederacy to save the contents of their chamber pots, from which nitre could be extracted. By the summer of 1862, the miracle had been worked: 'Where three years ago we were not making a gun nor a sabre, no shot nor shell (except at the Tredegar Works), nor a pound of powder,' boasted Josiah Gorgas, ' we now make all these in quantities to meet the demands of our large armies.'

But though more than capable of keeping their troops armed, the Confederates had a hard time keeping them fed. The South's economy had been dominated for decades by cotton. Land was replanted with food crops, but at nothing like the rate that was required. Those parts of the Confederacy that produced livestock and grain were in the upper South, Tennessee for example, and supplies from these areas were disrupted early in the war when the Union's armies invaded. As the war progressed, more and more of the country fell into Northern hands, and with it an ever-larger share of the Confederacy's food supply. But the single most important cause of food shortages, which affected soldiers and civilians alike, was the blockade of Southern ports set up by the Federal fleet. Food riots occurred in 1863, most notably in Richmond. One of the biggest causes of desertion from the rebel armies was concern for loved ones, starving on the home front. Though never totally effective, the blockade put enormous pressure on the South; the Confederacy, it might be argued, was starved into submission.

In contrast, the Northern people and their armies suffered no shortages. Some foreign war correspondents were amazed at the abundance of supplies (some of them, in their opinion, mere luxuries) that the Northern armies took on campaign. The West and Northwest were abundant in cattle and grain. No blockading ships prevented the steady flow of goods through its ports. Indeed, so rich did the Northern states become in foodstuffs that when poor harvests in Europe created a shortage, its exports of wheat quadrupled. This was the start of an important change in the relations between Europe and the United States. Hitherto the South had been the significant trading partner; that role now passed to the North.

Political Leadership

The opposing sides were led by administrations graced with very different capabilities. In time, Lincoln would prove a leader of greatness, though contemporaries would have predicted quite otherwise at the beginning of the war.

The South

The Confederate president, Jefferson Davis, greeted his appointment with dismay. His wife recalled how when he received the news of his election they were trimming rosebushes in the garden of their Mississippi home, and he looked as distraught as though a relative had died. He had a waspish temperament; in cabinet meetings and counsels of war he was quick to take offence when disagreed with. He suffered from neuralgia, which left him blind in one eye, sleeplessness and irritable bowel syndrome – all signs of the extreme stress under which he worked and of an innate irritability of temperament. Having selected men for his cabinet he seemed incapable of leaving them to get on with their jobs. Which may have been just as well, for the majority of men he appointed proved incompetent. In four years the Confederacy had as many Secretaries of War; in part because of public complaint about the course of the war, in part because of Davis's interfering and restive temperament. After a few months he was barely on speaking terms with his vice-president, Alexander H Stephens, who despised Davis for his allegedly illiberal and centralising conduct of the war. Stephens represented a faction who deplored the 'tyrannous' war measures promoted by the president: conscription, extraordinary forms of taxation and the suspension of habeas corpus (permitting arrest without trial of draft dodgers and those suspected of pro-Union activities). Davis lacked the tact and diplomacy needed to convince them of the necessity of such wartime 'tyranny', and the Confederate war effort was crippled by persistent dissent among its leaders.

Davis was a West Point graduate, had fought with distinction in the Mexican War and had served as Secretary of War for the United States. On the face of it, he seemed just the man for the job of leading the newly formed nation in a war. It was thanks to him that the South mobilised so rapidly and effectively in the months following secession. However, overestimating his military gifts, he often (and disastrously) interfered with his generals. Davis insisted on maintaining control of overall strategy - a task that should have devolved on someone more competent, someone who was not at the same time attempting to discharge the duties

29

of the government's chief executive. His inability to command loyalty and respect meant that what good ideas he had were not effectively realised, so little faith did his generals have in his judgment. Incoherent and vacillating, the Confederacy's grand strategy ill-served the men who fought, and died, trying to carry it out – and for this, Davis must bear much of the blame.

Many first-rate generals found themselves unable to put their talents to good use because of personal conflict with the president. Joseph E Johnston, veteran of the Mexican War, and one of the top-ranking professionals in the Union army, was angry when, soon after jointly winning the war's first major battle, he found Davis had made four other generals his seniors in rank. Davis's rancorous response to his complaint caused a rift that was never healed, though Johnston continued to occupy high military office, including commander in chief of the West from 1863. Another able but sadly under-utilised general was the man graced with a name that is redolent with Southern gallantry and charm (qualities on which he self-consciously prided himself): Pierre Gustave Toutant Beauregard. Johnston's joint commander at Bull Run, he fell foul of Davis because of a misunderstanding caused by Southern newspapers. They mistakenly reported Beauregard as claiming that Davis was responsible for the failure to pursue the defeated Union forces after the battle, thus losing a chance of occupying Washington. Thereafter, Davis transferred Beauregard to a subordinate position in the Confederate western armies; he ended the war in a command well below his abilities, overseeing the coastal defences of the Carolinas.

In the decades after the war, no one was so vilified by Southerners - not even General Sherman - as Jeff Davis; his tyrannical and bungling leadership had cost them the war, it was said. Yet no one could criticise his devotion to the cause. Even at the eleventh hour, when both Lee's and Johnston's armies had surrendered, he still fought on, attempting to transfer the government across the Mississippi River and join the small band of 'holdouts' under General Kirby Smith. Taken prisoner in Georgia, he spent two years in close confinement, spending part of the time in a cell kept fully illuminated round the clock. He was never tried. The last years of his life were spent in composing an impassioned account of secession and its justness. *The Rise and Fall of the Confederacy* is a powerful vindication of the right of states to secede, a paean to liberty that manages to ignore the fact of slavery.

The North

Few of its political and military leaders thought much of their new president in 1861. Lincoln's physical appearance provoked a mixed response. His figure was large and ungainly, his movements lacking in grace. He had prominent features, the nose and ears especially. This combination of large extremities and ungainliness led one of his generals, George B McClellan, to refer to him as 'the Gorilla'. The nickname also implied a low opinion of the president's intellect – a view common among Washington's elite. Lincoln's homespun wit was mistaken for rural idiocy, and the subtle and indirect way he had of addressing contentious issues so as not to commit himself unwisely, as a lack of coherence and purpose. A political novice, having sat only briefly in the House of Representatives, he had spent most of his career practising law. Davis and he were born within a few miles of each other, in Kentucky; the former the son of a wealthy slave owner, the latter that of an impoverished and itinerant farmer. Though his father-in-law owned slaves, Lincoln always detested the 'peculiar institution'. Believing in a society that rewarded on the basis of individual merit and effort, not birthright and privilege, Lincoln considered the democratic experiment in government a divine vocation assigned to the American people. They had been chosen to show the world that 'government by the people, of the people and for the people' was viable. 'The issue embraces more than the fate of these United States,' he wrote. 'It presents to the whole family of man the question, whether a constitutional republic, or democracy... can or cannot maintain its territorial integrity against its own domestic foes.'

Though against slavery, Lincoln was at first cautious in his approach. Radical abolitionists deplored his moderate attitude. In pre-war speeches he had said that he thought slavery would inevitably disappear, certainly by the end of the century. He was wary of the scale of the problems likely to be created by an instantaneous act of emancipation, and doubted the willingness of the majority to endorse such a scheme. His immediate task, he thought, was to win the war and preserve the Union, and all other considerations must be subordinate to that dual goal. It was the course of the war, and a clearer understanding of what it would take to win, that led both Lincoln and the conservative majority in the North to a more radical approach. What had been expected to be a short conflict had turned into a protracted war. The South could only wage such a war because of its use of slave labour. In this way, as a means towards the ultimate goal of restoring the Union, abolition became accepted. Lincoln would only

31

make it a central war aim once he knew that the majority could see the necessity of it; though personally antagonistic to slavery, he was too much of a pragmatist to force abolition on the electorate, and encourage it to reject him and the war for the Union.

Lincoln had a gift for getting along with people. Having selected someone he considered fit for a given task, he gave him his full support, without subsequent interference. He could disagree with someone without losing the man's support. He did not stand on his pride in cabinet discussions or meetings with his generals. On one occasion, he visited the then commander in chief of the Union armies, George B McClellan (a small man with a Napoleonic self-image), and agreed to wait in the front parlour for the General's return. When McClellan eventually arrived, though informed the president had been waiting for sometime, he ignored him and went straight up to bed. Lincoln's secretary was furious. The president's only comment was: 'I would hold the reins of McClellan's horse if he will only bring us success.'

Lincoln insisted on being closely involved in the conduct of the war. He had no military background and his generals were vexed by his interference, but he demonstrated a sound strategic sense in the directives he issued. He repeatedly urged the commanders of his armies to work in concert, to co-ordinate their attacks so that the enemy would not be able to draw troops from one sector to meet challenges occurring in another. The wisdom of this was many times proved right. In spring 1862, for example, the major prize of New Orleans fell into the hands of the Federal naval commander, Admiral Farragut, because the 15,000 rebel soldiers stationed in the area had been called away to deal with the Union invasion of central Tennessee. In contrast to Davis, Lincoln rewarded successful generals and stood by them when the press and public turned hostile. When Grant appeared to be floundering before Vicksburg in the winter of 1862-3, Lincoln responded to calls for his dismissal by saying, 'I cannot spare this man; he fights.' And when he realised that Grant was the man to lead the Union war machine to victory, he gave him a free hand.

As a politician, Lincoln was an unknown quantity when he took office. He had won the Republican nomination for president because his absence of a track record made it easier for the potentially discordant elements of the recently formed party to close ranks. Some of the better-known Republicans, William H Seward among them, had alienated certain sections of the electorate. If Seward had been nominated, many would almost certainly have voted Democrat. The men Lincoln picked for his cabinet represented a cross-section of the Republican Party, and were men of outstanding ability; Edwin M Stanton, for example, transformed with War Department with his ruthless efficiency and intolerance of corruption. Among the men Lincoln chose were four former rivals for the presidential nomination. In the first months of its existence, Seward was considered to be the real power in the administration; this was Seward's own view as well. But so effectively did Lincoln work on and with his cabinet, that he soon had one of the most harmonious and effective cabinets in American history.

War Aims And Grand Strategy

The North

When Lincoln called for 75,000 three-month volunteers to suppress the rebellion after the fall of Fort Sumter, he and the majority of Northerners expected a limited war with limited aims. Hence the small size of the volunteer body requested – and only for three months. Extreme Republicans harbouring abolitionist ambitions may have hoped to use the war as an instrument of social revolution (to destroy the Cotton Kingdom and slavery), but for the majority the aim was simply to restore the Union, to reset the clock to before 20 December 1860 when South Carolina seceded. In his early speeches, Lincoln spoke of the seceding states as if their state legislatures, executives and local Federal installations (arsenals and forts) had fallen into the hands of an organised outlaw minority. This was in keeping with the North's preferred description of the conflict, as a 'rebellion', not a 'war'. For 'war' would imply the existence of two belligerents, each having the status of a nation – thus conceding the very independence it was attempting to suppress. Through his careful choice of words, Lincoln was also suggesting that there were limits to be observed in the means employed to defeat the Confederacy. Wholesale destruction of property and social institutions might be fitting in a war against a foreign country, but not in the suppression of a rebellion. But events were to transform the scope of the North's vision of the conflict in the direction of total war.

A concern for the role Britain and France might play was also an important element in how the war was conceptualised. As we shall see, the Confederacy pinned much of their hope for victory on being recognized by these two countries. Such recognition would naturally lead to intervention with a view to a negotiated settlement on the basis of separation. It was vital that Lincoln do all he could to diminish the grounds for acknowledging Southern independence. How the conflict was reported in foreign newspapers, and debated by British and French politicians, and what policies were consequently adopted, would be shaped substantially by the descriptive vocabulary employed. The battle of semantics was not a trivial one.

The North began the war to restore the status quo, to bring the seceded states back into the Union, with slavery still a part of their fabric. Abolition was not an original war aim. Anti-slavery sentiment was a minority concern. 56% of the popular vote in the states that stayed in the Union had gone to candidates other than Lincoln, to candidates whose stand on the future of slavery was very much more conservative than the Republicans, only a minority of whom, in any case, advocated abolition of slavery wherever it existed. The Republicans' principal rivals, the Democrats, drew their support from the many who feared the enormous social problems expected to be caused by freeing four million blacks. Racism was rife in many areas of the North; in the southern counties of Illinois and Indiana, even Republican voters supported retention of the Exclusion Laws, which forbad the immigration of blacks, free or slave. For Lincoln to commit the nation to a war dedicated to freeing the slaves would have been impossible.

Lincoln was also wary of the impact of abolition as a war aim on the pro-Union groups he believed existed in the Confederacy, and on the slaveholding states which stayed in the Union. In the seceded South, East Tennessee, western North Carolina and eastern Georgia – up-country regions inhabited by poorer yeoman farmers, largely without slaves – there resided, Lincoln believed, great reserves of pro-Union sentiment that, if handled right, would help bring the seceded states back into the fold. While in Missouri, Kentucky and Maryland, which had not voted for secession, there were plenty of slaveholders, and the fate of these border-states hung in the balance for the first months of the war. Kentucky attempted to avoid taking sides by declaring neutrality, while Maryland's capital city, Baltimore, greeted the first troops to respond to Lincoln's call for volunteers by attacking them. In Missouri, a pro-Southern legislature was defeated by the pro-Union majority among the people, and so saved for the Union. But none of these would have welcomed a war on slavery.

In a context shaped by these considerations, the grand strategy evolved by General Scott was expressly designed to inflict limited damage on the South; rebel armies and points of major strategic importance were the target, not the people and their 'domestic institutions' (a common euphemism for slavery). Scott argued against waging war on the seceded states in such a way as to render them destitute – they would, after all, at some point be once again a part of the family of states. So he suggested to Lincoln what the Northern press derisively called the 'Anaconda Plan'. This involved cutting the Confederacy off from the outside world and its trade by means of a naval blockade, closing its land borders with troops, and driving a wedge down the Mississippi River to cut it in two. Using minimal force, he intended starving the rebels into submission. It drew flak from the press because, in the heady days when war first broke out, people were eager to get to grips with the rebels - partly because of the emotional tension that had built up over the preceding months, partly because it was widely believed that the issue could be settled by a single and decisive encounter on the battlefield. Further, the longer the rebel republic remained in existence, the more chance of foreign recognition. As it turned out, Scott's plan, implemented with exactly the ruthlessness he had wished to avoid, became the basis for Union victory.

Putting the blockade into position was a major undertaking, and proved to be one of the North's most striking successes. At the start of the war, the navy was pitifully small. The fleet consisted of forty-two ships, most of which were at the time patrolling waters remote from the Atlantic seaboard. The Confederate coastline was 3,500 miles long, comprising ten major ports and 180 inlets, bays and river mouths. In July 1861 a mere three-dozen ships constituted the blockade, and most of their time was spent travelling to and from the Union's two supply bases, Key West in Florida, and Hampton Roads in Virginia, to maintain stocks of fuel and food. By the spring of 1862 things were very different. Over three hundred ships were on blockade duty, rising to five hundred by the end of the year. Key points all along the coast fell into Federal hands: Port Royal, South Carolina; the Hatteras Inlet, North Carolina; and, forming the basis for operations in the Gulf of Mexico, Ship Island. The impact on the South's ability to wage war was considerable, both its armies in the field and its civilian population being pushed to the verge of starvation. Common foodstuffs, such as salt, became impossible to obtain; the price of flour rocketed. The food riots in 1863 throughout the South were the outcome of shortages brought on by the blockade. In the four-year period leading up to the war, 20,000 vessels had passed through Southern ports; in the war years, a mere 8,000 visited, and these were blockade-runners, built for speed not carrying capacity.

The Emergence Of Abolition As A War Aim

Beginning as a war for the restoration of the ante-bellum Union, it became a war for, in Lincoln's words, 'a new birth of freedom', a complete reconstruction of the Union, with the South's 'peculiar institution', and the way of life it underpinned, destroyed. How did this transformation come about? One reason was the response of the slaves; as soon as blue-coated troops began appearing on Southern soil, slaves fled to their encampments. This posed a problem, for the right to property in slaves was still officially a part of the Constitution, and unless the slaves were being used in belligerent activities, it was thought they should be returned to their rightful owners. But General Benjamin Butler, the Federal commander in 1861 of a small invasion force on the Yorktown Peninsular, east of Richmond, took a different view, and his response set a precedent. When a Virginia slave-owner requested the return of his property, Butler said the slaves were 'contrabands of war', refused to give them up, and put them to work driving teams and preparing fortifications. In time, and as the South's resistance stiffened with each passing month, Northerners came to believe that abolition was necessary to undermine its ability to go on with the fight. Slaves were routinely used by the rebels in a range of auxiliary duties, as cooks, teamsters and navvies. More important, however, black farmhands took over the work of whites, enabling them to enlist. For every slave taken from his master, one Illinois soldier mused in his diary, a rebel soldier was effectively rendered hors de combat; and to that degree, while unwilling to die for abolition per se, he was committed to freeing the blacks. The milestone in this transformation was Lincoln's Emancipation Proclamation of September 1862.

Lincoln, though fierce in his private condemnation of slavery, adopted a public policy in the first year of the war that reflected his pragmatic assessment of what was attainable. He well realised how unpopular a war for the freeing of the blacks would be. Further, he had the peoples of the three border-states, Missouri, Maryland and Kentucky – all slave states – to consider. He did not want to stampede these into the ranks of the seceded states, or feed their latent reservations about fighting a war to restore the Union. Consequently, much of the spring and summer of 1862 he spent trying to coax the slaveholding pro-Union states into voluntary emancipation, offering financial compensation from the state treasury. But their complete lack of response, and the increasing bitterness of the war, which was radicalising popular opinion, led him to abandon his 'softly softly' approach. When a decisive victory at the battle of Antietam, in September 1862, gave him the opportunity, he announced the freeing of all slaves in the rebel states, effective from 1 January 1863.

The South

Given the sheer scale of the North's economy, was the Confederacy, from the first, a forlorn hope? Not in the opinion of informed contemporary observers: 'It is one thing,' wrote *The Times* in 1861, ' to drive the rebels from the south bank of the Potomac [northern boundary of Virginia], or even to occupy Richmond, but another to reduce and hold in permanent subjection a tract of country nearly as large as Russia in Europe.... No war of independence ever terminated unsuccessfully except where the disparity of force was far greater than it is in this case.... Just as England during the revolution had to give up the colonies so the North will have to give up conquering the South.' To Jeff Davis and his government, the Revolutionary War was an example of how they might succeed. The odds had been stacked far more heavily against the Founding Fathers. Lincoln's administration faced a daunting military task, the subjugation of a territory virtually the same size as had confounded Napoleon's campaign of 1812; and the military capacity and expertise of the North did not seem, in spring 1861, anything remotely comparable to the Grand Armee of the French emperor. The South had merely to resist invasion, taking advantage of interior lines to move troops from place to place so as to even up the imbalance in numbers. In the process, they hoped to inflict heavy losses on the Union and wear away its will to fight. But in addition to the fruits of a defensive strategy, the Confederacy was also counting on foreign intervention. They believed that Europe was so dependent economically on the supply of Southern cotton that it would coerce the North, one way or another, into agreeing to disunion. On a number of occasions, Britain and France were, indeed, on the brink of doing just that.

In the autumn of 1861, in the aftermath of the Union defeat at Bull Run, the British government seriously considered recognising Southern independence, and intervening to stop hostilities. Sympathy for the Confederate cause was widespread among the British middle and upper classes. Conservative elements eagerly anticipated the collapse of America's experiment in radical democracy, which would help them in the struggle against universal suffrage being fought in Britain. Furthermore, the popular image of Northerners as brazen, Yankee upstarts made the prospect of their resounding defeat very appealing. Radicals like Gladstone and Bright favoured the Southerners in part because they thought of them as the spiritual kin of other oppressed minorities fighting for freedom from tyranny in Europe: the Italians, the Czechs and the Poles. While the North was protecting its nascent industries by imposing import duties, the South opposed such obstacles to free trade. At the time, the doctrine of free trade was the lynchpin of progressive thinking in Europe; when combined with nationalism and a moderate form of democracy it was deemed the panacea of the world's ills. For this reason, Gladstone and Bright could laud the South's advocacy of 'freedom', despite its four million slaves. All this was to be changed once the Emancipation Proclamation made abolition one of the North's professed war aims. After September 1862, no self-respecting European radical could blithely talk about the Confederacy's war for freedom.

Apart from his country's need of Southern cotton, Napoleon III of France had other, imperial, motives for favouring the Confederacy. He wanted to exploit Mexico's instability, and turn it into a satellite state under the nominal rule of his cousin, the Hapsburg Maximilian. French troops overthrew the Mexican government and installed Maximilian as emperor, at the head of an unstable regime. Napoleon held out to the Confederacy the prospect of assistance, in return for its support of the new order in Mexico. But he was never ready to take the initiative, preferring to let his British allies set the pace of foreign diplomacy. The success of his imperial ambitions, and of intervention on behalf of the South, depended on the route across Atlantic waters, which was controlled by Her Majesty's navy.

In fact, all parties overestimated the importance of Southern cotton, and of the impact of its loss. Other sources of supply were found to replace the South, and, of still greater significance, the global economy was in the process of restructuring: textiles were yielding to iron and steel as the dominant commodities. A vast stock of Southern cotton had been built up in British warehouses in the years immediately preceding the war, and these did not start to run out until mid-1862; by this time Egypt and India had begun to emerge as alternative sources of supply. The hardship that hit British textile workers in late 1862 was caused not by shortage of cotton, but by a surplus of cloth, glutting the market. The demand for textiles was on the decline, that for iron, steel and related forms of manufacture, enjoying a boom. In addition, the North became an important market for all kinds of goods necessary to its war effort. Losses in one sector of the economy due to the crisis in textiles were offset by gains in others, indirectly and directly stimulated by the war.

Among workers, even in the textile industry, there was little respect for the Confederacy. Emigration in the decades before the war had established strong ties with the Northeast and Northwest, where British and Irish workers settled in great numbers. Few found a livelihood in the South, however, for an economy dominated by slave labour offered little opportunity. The natural sympathies of working- and lower-middle classes were with the Union. Lincoln fully realised this. When a group of textile workers in Manchester wrote in the autumn of 1862 to reassure him of their support in spite of the hardships apparently brought on by the Northern blockade, he was at pains to register his appreciation of their support. Though a pragmatist in the framing of policy, Lincoln was never less than an idealist in his overall conception of the war's purpose; it was being fought to vindicate an idea of world-historic significance. When workers in Britain acknowledged that their fate was implicated in the outcome of the war, it confirmed his faith in its divinely ordained purpose.

Several crises came close to precipitating the foreign intervention hoped for by the South. In November 1861, two Southern envoys, Mason and Slidell, set off for Europe, first by way of a blockade-runner to Cuba, transferring there onto HMS Trent, bound for Liverpool. An enterprising US naval officer decided to intercept the ship and confiscate the two envoys as 'contrabands of war' – which he duly did. Her Majesty's government exploded in fury and British troops were sent to Canada in preparation for war. For a month tension between the two governments was at breaking point. But Lincoln wisely decided to back down ('One war at a time,' he said), and Mason and Slidell were set free.

On three subsequent occasions, the British and French governments came close to recognition, each time in response to the successes of Southern arms: when Lee invaded the North, first in autumn 1862 and then in summer 1863, and when General Grant's vast army was embroiled in a bloody and apparently fruitless siege outside the Southern town of Petersburg in summer and winter of 1864. Southern military strategy, though largely defensive, evolved to incorporate offensive components whose purpose was to elicit foreign intervention and demoralise the Northern electorate.

Waging war on the South was never uniformly popular among the Northern states. As has been pointed out, a majority of the electorate did not vote for Lincoln, and there was a lot of sympathy for the Southern view that the election of the 'Black Republican', with his radical, pro-abolition following, had precipitated the war, that the South had merely pre-empted Republican-led aggression. The high number of casualties, and the protracted and doubtful progress of the war, dragging on from one year to the next, caused many to lose heart in the policy of restoring the Union through violent means. The abolition issue stirred up mixed responses. Initially, the ordinary Northerner was adamant that he was not going to die for 'any damn niggers'. The needs of the situation convinced him otherwise. Yet right through the conflict, a sufficient number of citizens could be roused into anti-Lincoln, anti-war frenzy by demagogues, mostly Democrats attempting to win votes, denouncing the war as a crusade on behalf of the blacks. Confederate offensives were timed to coincide with the national and state elections, in the hope that anti-war Democrats would win the support of a war-weary electorate, and call a ceasefire.

Lee's two invasions were intended to influence the outcome of congressional elections. His dogged opposition to Grant in 1864 was designed to wreck Lincoln's chances for re-election in the autumn - which it very nearly did. Throughout the spring and summer the Democrats were gaining support on the basis of a promise of peace. Only an accident of timing prevented Lincoln's defeat. Had the election been due in August instead of November he would almost certainly have lost.

Part Three: The War

Overview

The South was defeated by a version of the 'Anaconda Plan' of General Scott, the main variation consisting in the ruthlessness with which Grant and Sherman implemented it. There were two principal theatres of war: the eastern, stretching from the Atlantic coast to the ridge of the Appalachian Mountains that run northeast-southwest; and the western, comprising the lands west of the Appalachians to the Mississippi River and beyond.

Jeff Davis took the sensible course of appointing one commanding general for each of the two theatres: initially, Albert Sidney Johnston for the west, and Joseph E Johnston for the east. A. S. Johnston, considered a general of great promise, was one of the few commanders Davis ever trusted. Unfortunately, he was killed at the battle of Shiloh within a few months of the beginning of serious campaigning in the west. Thereafter, the Confederacy's western command was hampered by dissent among its generals and frequent changes in leadership. Davis appointed generals whose efforts he undermined by his interference and lack of trust. The eastern theatre fared better in this respect. After the first ten months, it passed into the hands of Robert E Lee, a military figure of legendary aspect.

Graduate of West Point, veteran of the Mexican War, Lee was serving as a colonel in Texas when secession erupted in the winter of 1860-1. A Virginian and owner of a large number of slaves, he professed an abhorrence of secession and slavery. General Scott recommended that supreme command of the Union forces be given him, and the offer was made on the day Lee's native state joined the Confederacy. Despite a lifetime spent in the service of the Federal government, he resigned his commission and accepted an appointment as Brigadier General of Volunteers in the Confederate army. Like many Southerners, he considered his home state as having prior claim on his allegiance; he always referred to Virginia as his 'country'. A man of deep religious conviction, courtly in manner, and not prone to displays of emotion, he was ruthless as a commander, ready to gamble very high stakes on manoeuvres considered the height of folly according to the textbooks – manoeuvres whose success was achieved at considerable cost to his own men. The units in his army – the Army of Northern Virginia – suffered 43% casualty rates during the course of the war, a higher percentage than any other force on either side.

At Gettysburg, he ordered an assault by fifteen thousand men across exposed ground against enemy protected by breastworks and supported by artillery; seven thousand fell in the space of an hour. Despite this his men never wavered in their devotion, and the Southern newspapers hailed even his bloodiest battles without demur, though casualty rates of a lower order led the press in the North to tag Grant with the soubriquet 'The Butcher'. On several occasions, he divided his already outnumbered force in the face of the enemy to execute a bold flanking movement, soundly beating his astonished opponent as a result. As he led them from victory to victory, he bred in the hearts of his troops a fanatical devotion to 'Marse Robert'.

The phases of the war were, briefly, as follows. In the eastern theatre, fighting was concentrated in Virginia, where Union armies made repeated attempts to fight their way to the Confederate capital, Richmond. The two capitals were less than two hundred miles apart. For four years, the opposing forces surged north and south across the state, Lee twice breaking through its northern border and invading the Union, first into Maryland in 1862, then into Pennsylvania in 1863. The nature of the war underwent a significant transformation in spring of 1864, when Grant assumed supreme command of the Federal forces, basing his HQ with the Union's eastern force, the Army of the Potomac. Whereas previous Northern generals had moved against Lee, fought, been defeated and withdrawn to lick their wounds, Grant, no matter the outcome of individual battles, did not let up. Under Grant, the Army of the Potomac just kept on fighting. After ten months of continual campaigning, this policy paid off. An exhausted Army of Northern Virginia gave up its defence of Richmond and neighbouring Petersburg, fleeing west to Appomattox Courthouse, scene of Lee's surrender to Grant.

In the western theatre, the war really begins in February 1862. The first five months are a series of remarkable successes. Federal forces advance into the Mississippi valley from both North and South; by June, the northern boundary of effective Confederate power has been driven back to the upper reaches of Mississippi and Alabama, and the two halves of the Confederacy – separated by the Mississippi – are linked by a mere two-hundred-mile stretch centred on the town of Vicksburg. The Union invasion then grinds to a halt for nearly a year, during which Grant makes repeated attempts to take Vicksburg and so complete the slicing through of the Confederacy. After the fall of Vicksburg in July 1863, Union armies move gradually east, getting held up once again, this time around Chattanooga in southeast Tennessee. The final phase begins with the investment of Atlanta in late summer 1864 – by which time Sherman has taken over as commander in the West. Following its fall, Sherman begins his famous 'March to the Sea', turning north along the Atlantic coast in the winter of 1864-5 to link up with Grant's army. Joseph E Johnston, commanding the remnants of the Confederacy's western army – the Army of Tennessee – surrenders to Sherman a few weeks after Lee.

From Bull Run To The Peninsula Campaign 1861-2

Baptism Of Fire: Bull Run

General Beauregard had, after a thirty-six hour bombardment, costing the life of one army mule, forced Federal Fort Sumter to surrender. A jubilant South was eager to follow up this victory and bring the war to a swift conclusion. The North, for its part, was just as keen to expunge the opprobrium of this early setback, and give the rebels a pummelling. Neither side had any idea how long a conflict it was going to be – nor how costly. A holiday atmosphere marked the start of the war, and everyone was eager to claim his share of glory in battle. Volunteers on both sides turned up in numbers that outstripped the supplies of guns and uniforms. Men fretted at the slow pace of mobilisation, worrying that the war would be over before they finished their basic training.

Though called on to defend a national cause, troops were recruited and equipped largely through the initiative of local effort, and there was, as a result, little standardisation in the appearance of the first wave of volunteers. The 37th New York wore a uniform modelled on the French North African Zouaves, with baggy red trousers, fringed waistcoat and red fez. Other Northern units, reflecting their ethnic origins, wore tartan and kilts. Millionaire South Carolinian, Wade Hampton, kitted out his 'legion' – a unit of one thousand infantry, cavalry and artillery, recruited and paid for out of his own pocket – according to his own flamboyant notions of military dress. Plumes and braid abounded. Although in time a uniform code of dress would be adopted – grey for the South, and the regular army blue for the North – when they first came to blows many units were dressed in similar colours. In more than one fight in the first year, foe was mistaken for friend, and vice versa, with catastrophic results. Even the two battle flags were similar in design, the Southern 'Stars and Bars' being indistinguishable in the smoke of battle from the Northern 'Stars and Stripes'.

By July 1861 a Federal force of 35,000 had mustered on the banks of the Potomac River outside Washington, at its head the cautious and ill-fated professional soldier, General Irwin McDowell. Twenty miles south, at Manassas Junction, were 25,000 Confederate troops under General Beauregard. This was an important rail junction, lying at the intersection of the main north-south line and the east-west route to the Shenandoah Valley. Lying to the west, the Valley was a key strategic location, serving both as a granary to the South and as a natural and easily protected route for invasion Northwards. Debouching from the funnel of the Valley, a rebel army could easily circle around Washington, cutting its rail links to the north and west. The northern capital's close proximity to the Confederacy made it especially vulnerable to attack – indeed it was surrounded by a state, Maryland, which many considered a part of Dixie. Stationed at Harper's Ferry, at the northern end of the Valley, General Pattison, with 12,000 men, had been allotted the job of tackling the nearby force of 15,000 rebel troops under General Johnston. Though wary of committing his raw recruits to battle, McDowell was urged by Lincoln to move on the rebels at Manassas; if the Union men were ill prepared, Lincoln pointed out, the same was equally true of the Confederates.

The success of the plan formulated by McDowell depended on his colleague, Pattison. He intended to attack Beauregard's forces, which were drawn up on the southern side of a small river called Bull Run, by making a diversionary assault on the enemy's front, while sending a column on a wide flanking march to make the real assault on his left and rear. At all costs, Pattison had to prevent Johnston's troops from using the rail link to join Beauregard, which would rob McDowell of the numerical advantage on which the success of his plan was predicated. This he failed to do. Unsure of his raw recruits' response to combat, he kept them too far from the rebel positions, and Beauregard was able to take his men east to Johnston. At 2 am on 21 July, McDowell's flanking column set off on its twelve-mile march. The plan called for it to hit the rebels soon after dawn, but when the sun came up it was still struggling along the narrow back roads north of the river. By the time it launched its attack at ten o'clock, Johnston's troops were already beginning to disembark at Manassas Junction. Initially, however, the rebel left had a hard time of it, being driven back from their original position to a piece of high ground called Henry House Hill. It was around this hill that, through the space of seven hours, Americans got their first taste of what was to come. Twenty-five thousand men on each side were engaged in a struggle for the hill. Wave after wave of Federal troops crashed against the rebel line, which, though shaken, managed to stand its ground. But when it came under the murderous fire of enemy batteries stationed close by, it began to falter. It was at this point that the commander of one of the brigades in the rebel line earned his nickname, 'Stonewall'. A fellow brigade commander, attempting to rally his men, urged them to emulate the Virginians under General Jackson, who were standing firm as a stonewall. The Union batteries that had caused all the trouble fell victim to the lack of standardisation in uniform. They mistook an approaching regiment, dressed in regulation army blue, for supporting Union troops, and were shot down at close range by Confederates who had worked their way around their flank. As more and more Valley troops arrived, the rebels built up sufficient numbers to launch a counter attack; by late afternoon, the Union forces were on the run.

People were appalled at the scale of the losses: 500 to 600 killed, and 1200 wounded, on each side. In addition, the North lost 1200 as prisoners. McDowell's army fled headlong – accompanied by scores of terrified civilians who had, earlier in the day, flocked to the scene with picnic hampers to enjoy the spectacle of a grand battle - pausing only once it had reached the streets of Washington, by now a disorganised rabble. But the armies of Johnston and Beauregard had been thrown into almost as great a state of confusion by their victory as the Federals had by their defeat, and no pursuit was made. This failure to capitalise on their victory at Bull Run was to be viewed by Southerners as one of their leaders' great blunders.

'Little Mac' And The Army Of The Potomac: The Peninsula Campaign

A week after the defeat at Bull Run, Lincoln called for half a million three-year volunteers – a sign that the true scale of the conflict was beginning to be acknowledged. That week he also summoned General George B McClellan from his successful, if minor, campaigning in West Virginia, to take charge of the battered fragments of McDowell's forces and to mould them, together with a continuing flow of raw recruits, into a new force - the Army of the Potomac.

Thirty-four years old and a professional soldier with an enviable reputation, McClellan made a strong and positive impact on arrival in Washington. One contemporary remarked: 'There is an indefinable air of success about him and something of the man of destiny.' Styling himself on Napoleon (photographs show him in the Emperor's customary pose, one hand disappearing beneath the breast-pocket of his coat), McClellan set about turning one hundred thousand men into a disciplined army. He organised the camps around the capital, held grand parades, and drilled his men constantly, restoring their pride and self-confidence. Grateful for his efforts on their behalf and as a token of their affection, his men dubbed him 'Little Mac'. In those first months McClellan earned the love and respect of the army, and, despite all that subsequently happened, he was never to lose it. But while he was an excellent creator of armies, McClellan seemed reluctant to put them to their intended use. Inclined to be over-anxious about the enemy's intentions and numbers, McClellan allowed himself to be frozen into immobility by what he thought the Confederates were about to do to him. He was never quite ready to commit his forces to the test of battle. There was always some further piece of preparation necessary, or – and this was more often the case – the numbers were not quite right, and he needed another twenty or thirty thousand troops if he was to engage the enemy on an equal footing. In fact, at most times, he outnumbered the Confederates by at least two to one.

As summer turned to autumn, Lincoln grew increasing alarmed at McClellan's failure to act. The rebels were still encamped within twenty miles of the capital, and the Army of the Potomac showed no signs of making a move before settling in to winter quarters. He had not enough men, McClellan said, to wage a campaign, the rebels under Johnston numbering a hundred thousand. In fact, Johnston had fewer than half that number. Feeding McClellan's paranoia were the ineptly prepared reports of his intelligence network, headed by William Pinkerton.

Lincoln insisted that he strike the rebels encamped at Manassas. Instead he came up with a plan to ship his vast army down the coast, and land it at the end of the Yorktown Peninsula, and from there to send it the short distance west, inland to Confederate capital, Richmond. This plan had the advantage that his supply line, being by sea, would be invulnerable to rebel attack, and that, on its way to Richmond, the army would have to cross but two rivers – instead of the countless rivers it would encounter on a route due south from Washington. But as Lincoln pointed out, when McClellan got to the Peninsula he would still have to fight the same forces as were presently a little way south from Washington; still, happy to have got at least some movement out of his general, Lincoln agreed to the plan.

The campaign on the Peninsula lasted the spring of 1862, and was, thanks to McClellan, a disaster. He moved his vast army at a snail's pace, allowing the rebels to withdraw their forces south to meet him and to prepare heavy defences outside Richmond and at Yorktown, a few miles inland from the landing point of the Union army. So convinced was he of the rebels' strength in numbers, that McClellan allowed himself to be bamboozled by one of Johnston's generals, John B Magruder, commanding a force at Yorktown, into believing that his fifteen thousand men were many times that number. Magruder, a devotee of amateur theatricals, put on a terrific show of force; regiments were repeatedly marched in and out of the same forest clearings to give the impression of vast numbers being grouped for an assault, while the artillery was spread thinly over many miles to make it seem the rebel position positively bristled with cannons. After a month of preparation, McClellan's advance force of fifty-five thousand, supported by countless pieces of heavy artillery and mortars, prepared to assault the rebels, but on the night before the day of the attack Magruder quietly slipped back to the defences outside Richmond.

But it was here that the two armies at last came to grips in a bloody encounter, at Seven Forks, which cost each side five thousand dead and wounded, and left the two lines exactly where they had been before fighting began. This encounter did achieve one important result, however. The rebel commander, Johnston, was severely wounded, and Davis chose for his replacement the man who had been acting as his special military adviser: Robert E Lee. It was the beginning of Lee's control of the Confederate war effort in the east.

Lee fully appreciated McClellan's weaknesses, and he decided to exploit them by playing upon Lincoln's fears for the safety of his capital. The defence of Washington was of paramount importance to the president, and in working out the plans for McClellan's campaign, Lincoln had been at pains to ensure that adequate numbers were held back in northern Virginia to deal with any rebel threat emanating from the Shenandoah Valley. McClellan had taken up a position outside Richmond that straddled a river called the Chickahominy, extending his right wing in anticipation of extra troops coming south with McDowell – troops without which McClellan did not think he had sufficient numbers to undertake the siege of Richmond. Lee planned to deny McClellan those extra troops by playing on Lincoln's fear of the Valley, and thus bring the advancing Union juggernaut to a standstill.

The task of panicking Lincoln into keeping McDowell's men away from the Peninsula was given to General 'Stonewall' Jackson. The Valley Campaign, as it is known, was Jackson's finest achievement. He took his brigades to the Shenandoah Valley and proceeded to run rings around three separate Union armies, reaching as far north as Harper's Ferry. Lincoln responded as Lee had anticipated, and McClellan was denied the extra troops he had been counting on. In the space of a month, Jackson fought and won five major engagements, marched his men over four hundred miles and captured hundreds of tons of badly needed supplies. Though his force numbered a mere seventeen thousand he fought and defeated Union armies with a combined strength of thirty-three thousand.

Jackson drove his men hard – he called them his 'foot cavalry'. He showed little pity for the enemy or, for that matter, for his own men; in battle he seemed indifferent to death and suffering, his own or that of others. He was a hard leader and ruthless fighter; this brought him many victories that earned him the profound respect, but not the love, of his troops. A true eccentric, he rode with his left arm raised so as to maintain the balance of the blood, refused to season his food with pepper because he believed it made his leg ache, and sucked constantly on lemons, even in battle. Men claimed to see a blue light illuminate his eyes when the fighting started. Psychopath he may have been, but his service to Lee was of incalculable benefit; more often than not, Lee entrusted his most audacious tactical manoeuvres to Jackson. Lee's defeat at Gettysburg was in large part due to the fact that he was without his most trusted lieutenant, Jackson having died a few weeks earlier at the battle of Chancellorsville.

Having delayed McClellan's advance by sending Jackson to the Valley, Lee set to work preparing a counterattack. He strengthened the defensive positions outside Richmond, south of the Chickahominy River, intending to hold them with a fraction of his force. He planned to concentrate superior numbers against the Union corps north of the river, ordering Jackson to rush his troops from the Valley and fall on the flank and rear of the Union right. In early June began seven days of almost continuous fighting. The first assault against the Union right did not go well for the rebels. The attack was poorly co-ordinated, and Jackson moved his troops as if through molasses. Jackson's lacklustre performance was in striking contrast to the energy he had shown the previous month. It is possible he was suffering from complete physical prostration – his subordinates reported that he nodded off to sleep even in the midst of the fighting. Whatever the cause, his failure was one of the chief reasons for the rebels losing four of the five major engagements that week. The other main reason was the rebel army's complicated chain of command. There were no corps in the rebel army, so that Lee had to communicate his battle plans to eighteen different divisional commanders (divisions being the smaller units out of which corps are composed). Later he remedied this, creating two corps headed by Jackson and James Longstreet, thus consolidating the structure of the Army of Northern Virginia, helping to turn it into the flexible instrument of his will.

Though he had repulsed the rebels on the first day at Mechanicsville, McClellan decided to withdraw his right wing to a stronger position a few miles to the east at Gaines' Mill. But here the Union line, attacked once more, was shattered, its centre being broken by a brigade of Texans under the pugnacious John Bell Hood. The Union troops were forced to retreat south of the Chickahominy. Lee continued with a series of costly and unsuccessful attacks, at Savage's Station, White Oak Swamp and – most murderously – Malvern Hill, where the rebels charged a hill lined with over a hundred pieces of artillery. In the space of an hour five thousand Confederates fell in a hail of shrapnel and shell. During that week Lee kept on attacking because McClellan, despite suffering fewer losses and winning the battles, kept on retreating. True to form, he lost the campaign simply because he didn't have the heart for an all-out fight. Indeed, as soon as he decided to pull his right wing south of the Chickahominy he signalled Lee his decision to give up. His supply line had been based on the York River to the north, in part because the railroad ran from that direction south, and it was along this that the heavy siege artillery necessary for the reduction of Richmond would travel. Once he switched his supply base to the James River to the south, which he did as part of uniting the two wings of his army on the south side of the Chickahominy, he effectively abandoned all attempts at besieging the rebel capital; by no other approach could heavy artillery be brought to within range of Richmond.

Lincoln visited the Peninsula in late June to urge McClellan to resume the offensive. Fighting had come to a halt. Lee's army had been exhausted by its attacks, having suffered 25% casualties; the Union losses were half that of the rebels', only 10% of its fighting force. But McClellan said he needed more men, convinced still of the rebels' parity in numbers. 'If I gave him all he wanted,' Lincoln commented, 'there would only be enough room on the Peninsula for the Army of the Potomac to sleep standing up. And he would still ask me for more.' Lincoln gave up, and McClellan was allowed to take his men back North.

The West: Fall Of Forts Henry And Donelson, And The Battle Of Shiloh

Until the beginning of 1862, little of consequence occurred in the west. Along a front five hundred miles long Confederate General A S Johnston defended the Confederacy with seventy thousand troops. The left of his line was anchored on the Mississippi at Columbus, Kentucky, and stretched due east to the Appalachian Mountains. Down the Mississippi the rebels had a string of heavily fortified positions; Columbus itself had 140 guns – it was nicknamed the 'Gibraltar of the West' – while further south there lay forts at Island Number 10 and Memphis. Together, these appeared to make the Mississippi impregnable along the one hundred and forty mile stretch due south of Cairo, Illinois, the Union's southernmost stronghold in the region.

Next to the Mississippi itself, the most important strategic consideration in this area was Tennessee, lying to the south of Kentucky. Of enormous economic significance, Tennessee produced grain, mules and horses in abundance; the town of Clarksville was home to the Confederacy's second largest ironworks (it had only two), while Nashville was the main supply depot for the entire Confederate western army (known as the Army of Tennessee). The way into this vital region was provided by a pair of rivers, tributaries of the Mississippi, which flowed, first east and then south through Tennessee: the Tennessee and the Cumberland Rivers. Defending this route into the Confederate heartland, and lying at the centre of the extended rebel line of defence, were two forts: Fort Henry on the Tennessee, and Fort Donelson on the Cumberland. They were not a credit to Southern military engineering – especially Fort Henry, whose lower gun embrasures flooded when prolonged seasonal rains caused the river to rise. These were the weak point in the rebel line, but for a time the Federals could not co-ordinate their efforts to take advantage of it.

Along the same front, from the Appalachians to the Mississippi, the Union had one hundred and five thousand troops, divided between the commands of Generals Halleck and Buell. Lincoln constantly urged them to make contact with Johnston's troops and get the ball rolling, but Halleck and Buell were not about to be rushed. Hindered by their background as professional soldiers, they considered the taking of strategic positions, by means of carefully executed flanking movements, more important than engaging the enemy army in battle and defeating it. They were of that class of officers, Lincoln's bete noire, whose punctilious, textbook mentality was to prolong the struggle, and allow the Confederacy time to build up strength at home and support abroad. Further, Buell and Halleck were each jealous of their reputations and disinclined to assist the other in making a move on the enemy that might enhance his rival's career. Luckily for the Union, Halleck's second in command was Ulysses S Grant.

Before the war Grant had been working in his father's business in Illinois, having recently failed at farming. He had been at West Point and had fought in the Mexican War, but finding an army salary too small to support a family he had resigned his commission. In none of the business ventures he turned his hand to did he have any success. Whereas other Union professional soldiers were prone to posturing, holding grand parades and issuing showy proclamations to their troops, Grant was shabby, laconic and unpretentious. He had an unusually clear grasp of what was in his mind, and was extremely able at communicating it to others. After a particular battle, one officer noted with amazement, Grant sat down and wrote his reports and orders for further dispositions for two hours without a pause, translating into forceful and unambiguous prose what his intentions were. This was no mean accomplishment. Many senior officers relied on their staff for drafting their orders, and the use of vague and ambiguous wording was the cause of serious problems in more than one campaign.

But this clarity in respect of his own intentions, proceeding from a profound sense of determination, sometimes led him to underestimate his opponent. Before the battle of Shiloh, he was, by his own admission, so intent on the attack he was about to launch that it never occurred to him his opponent was planning the same thing – it was for this reason that the rebel attack was able to sweep through the Union encampments, unimpeded by even the flimsiest of breastworks. In the trenches before Petersburg, two years later, he snapped at one of his generals who was plaintively speculating about Lee's next move: 'I am heartily tired of hearing what Lee is going to do. Some of you always seem to think he is suddenly going to turn a double somersault, and land on our rear and on both our flanks at the same time. Go back to your command, and try to think what we are going to do ourselves, instead of what Lee is going to do.' His friend, General Sherman, remarked on his cool-headed determination, a quality noted by all who had anything to do with him. When he took charge in the east, his first forays against Lee were costly and by no means clear in their result. The men in the Army of the Potomac, used to the likes of McClellan and his successors, expected the order to retreat, and they were delighted when told simply to keep on advancing and attacking instead. Grant, they realised, would not concede defeat. His unshakeable will to win, percolating down into the armies he led, was one of the main causes of Union victory.

Grant persuaded Halleck to let him have a stab at Forts Henry and Donelson. Working in concert with a flotilla of gunboats under Flag Officer David Porter, Grant moved on Henry; before he could get his fifteen thousand troops into position, Porter's gunboats had reduced the fort to submission. The rebel commander, realising that he was vastly outnumbered, had evacuated the bulk of his garrison east to Fort Donelson. Johnston showed poor judgment in his response to this attack on the centre of his line. Military logic offered him a choice: either concentrate his forces at Donelson and make a real fight of it there, or withdraw the entire army, leaving a token force at the fort to delay the Federal advance. Instead he sent more than ten thousand to Donelson, and withdrew south, awaiting the outcome of Grant's attack. When Donelson fell to Grant's men, Johnston lost a considerable number of troops he could ill-afford and substantial supplies. He then proceeded to withdraw by stages from Clarksville, Nashville and from his fortified positions along the Mississippi, concentrating his troops around the key town of Corinth, in northern Mississippi. Here, he declared, the Confederate forces must hold; there could be no further withdrawal.

Unfairly taking credit for Grant's success, Halleck was promoted to overall command in the western theatre. He now instructed Grant to move south to a place called Pittsburgh Landing, on the Tennessee River, north of Corinth, to await the arrival of Buell; once united, the combined force of over one hundred thousand was to move against the rebels. Seeing his opportunity, Johnston decided to bring superior numbers to bear on Grant before Buell could join him. General Beauregard, Johnston's second-in-command, devised a complicated plan involving the rebel corps moving along four converging roads. Units got lost, divisions failed to move on time because of roads blocked by the baggage trains of other divisions, and raw recruits failed to keep in column and cover the distances stipulated in the plan. Despite a delay of nearly two days, by early Sunday morning, 6 April, Johnston had forty-two thousand troops in position opposite the Federal line, which stretched for two miles between a small creek and the Tennessee River. The region, gently undulant, was intersected by meandering dirt roads and creeks, and visibility was limited to a few hundred yards in any direction due to the large number of trees and a dense undergrowth. It was early spring, and the many apple and peach orchards in the vicinity were in blossom. When the grey-clad soldiers burst upon them, the Federal troops were taken completely by surprise, many of them still preparing breakfast. An inadequate picket line had been posted (thanks to Grant's preoccupation with his own plans for attack), and it was impossible to see the rebel battalions massing only a few hundred yards away.

Grant had only five of his six divisions available that day. The sixth, General Lew Wallace's (later the author of *Ben Hur*), spent the day wandering around off to the west, trying to make its way round to its appointed place on the right of the Union line. Of the remainder, Sherman and Prentiss's divisions were only recently arrived from the recruiting stations. Indeed few men on either side had seen any serious fighting. Sherman's troops held the centre of the Union line, along a ridge of ground on top of which was built the church of Shiloh. For Sherman it was the turning point of his career; for twelve hours he moved up and down the ranks, encouraging his men, rallying stragglers, and finding units to plug the rapidly appearing holes in his line. Twice wounded, he had three horses shot from under him. The shock of the rebel attack pushed the wings of Grant's line back two miles; but the centre, under General Prentiss, taking advantage of a sunken road, held on. The broken nature of the terrain, combined with the rawness of the troops, meant that attacks were made in separate forays of brigade-sized strength. For hours Prentiss and his men refused to yield any ground – four and a half thousand withstood the eighteen thousand rebels who assaulted them. Eventually, sixty-eight guns were lined up at close range, and shrapnel was poured into the Federal line. Having held up the rebel advance until nearly sunset, Prentiss and his men surrendered. There were a little over two thousand of them left.

During the afternoon, Johnston had been killed while rallying his troops near the centre to renew the attack. Though things had been going well for the Confederates, their officers were having a hard time convincing at least a portion of their raw recruits to go on with the fight. For many on both sides, the first sight of 'the elephant' (the veteran's euphemism for first combat experience) proved too great. Thousands of Confederates broke rank and ran; while the bluffs by the river behind the Union line were shelter for over five thousand troops who had fled their various commands. That night both lines rested fitfully within sight of each other, beneath a steady downpour of rain; the twelve square miles of the battlefield were littered with some two thousand dead and twelve thousand wounded.

The Confederate command passed to Beauregard, and he telegraphed Jefferson Davis with news of a great victory. He expected to finish the enemy off in the morning, he said. Unfortunately his cavalry had misinformed him of the progress of Buell's army. Unbeknownst to Bearegard, it was disembarking and getting into line that very night. Early next day, and now with overwhelming odds in his favour, Grant launched a counterattack. The battle raged from dawn until mid-afternoon; then the rebels disengaged and began a rapid retreat to their fortified positions in Corinth.

The total in killed and wounded on both sides was more than twenty thousand - more Americans than had been killed in all the country's previous wars combined. For Grant it was a revelation of the true nature of the conflict. Up to that point, he had expected the Confederacy to yield after one more decisive defeat: 'My opinion is,' he had written before Shiloh, 'that this war will be closed in less than six months.' But now he spoke of continuing 'in my country's service until this rebellion should be put down, should it be ten years.' He 'gave up all idea of saving the Union except by complete conquest.'

In contrast to its fortunes in the east, and despite the near catastrophe at Shiloh, in the west the North seemed to have everything going its way in the late spring and early summer of 1862. 50,000 square miles of territory had been taken, including a thousand miles of navigable river, two state capitals, the South's largest city (New Orleans, which had fallen to a naval expedition), and 30,000 enemy soldiers had been put out of action. The Confederates had withdrawn to the northern area of the state of Mississippi (though they continued to maintain a tenuous grip on east Tennessee), but were poised for further withdrawal; in May, due to increasing levels of sickness among his men, caused by its pestilential location and the summer heat, Beauregard decided to abandon Corinth. Only a two hundred-mile stretch of the Mississippi, with the major town of Vicksburg at its centre, held the two halves of the Confederacy together. But the rebels were on the brink of a spectacular come back.

From Manassas To The Winter Campaigns Of 1862-3

Lee's First Invasion Of The North

As McClellan's vast army boarded ships and began to sail north, General John Pope, a brash and pompous professional, fresh from minor successes in Missouri, arrived to take charge of Federal forces in northern Virginia. Lincoln instructed him to create a new army, the Army of Virginia, out of the forces recently bested by Jackson – the commands of Fremont, Banks and McDowell. Pope, Lincoln's advisers warned him, was a liar and a braggart, and not to be trusted. Lincoln replied that he saw no reason why a liar and a braggart should not make a good general. Pope liked to give the impression that he was a man of action, always in the field with his troops; it was his frequent boast that his headquarters was in his saddle. Critics interpreted this to mean that he had an arse for a brain – and circumstances proved them correct.

Lincoln hoped that his two northern armies (the Army of the Potomac and the Army of Virginia) and their commanders would co-operate in bringing to bear overwhelming odds against Lee. It was not to happen. McClellan felt piqued at being asked to work alongside a man he considered his inferior; officers, including senior generals, in his command felt the same. McDowell, smarting from his recent humiliation at the hands of Jackson, flinched at Pope's scathing comment that, in the west, Union troops were unaccustomed to seeing anything but the backs of their foes. Dissension among the senior Federal command was the crucial factor in the next Federal defeat.

To meet the threat posed by Pope, Lee sent Jackson with twenty-five thousand men northwards to Gordonsville. Seeing an opportunity, Jackson attacked an inferior force under the command of General Banks at Cedar Mountain and, after a sharp fight, hurled them back in confusion. Before Pope could bring up the rest of his army in support, Jackson had disappeared. Meantime, the first of McClellan's units were beginning to arrive from the Peninsula, and Pope was anxious not to engage the Confederates until he had increased the odds in his favour as much as possible by means of these additional troops. Lee arrived from the outskirts of Richmond, and gathered his fifty-five thousand – including Jackson's men – on the south bank of the Rappahanock River, in central Virginia. Seeing Pope inactive, Lee decided on one of his daring flanking manoeuvres. Although already outnumbered by Pope, Lee gauged correctly the character of his opponent, and he knew that bold and decisive action was not something to be expected of him. Lee sent Jackson's force on a long march twenty-five miles around Pope's army to attack its main supply point at Manassas Junction. With customary swiftness and stealth, Jackson's 'foot cavalry' moved on their target, ripping up miles of railroad, stealing hundreds of tons of food and ammunition, and destroying all they could not carry away. Jackson then withdrew a few miles west, and lined up his men in a defensive position along a disused railway cutting.

Pope's cavalry performed poorly as scouts. After the fight at Cedar Mountain they had lost track of Jackson, and once again they seemed unable to discover his whereabouts. The rebels' position at last uncovered, Pope instructed his corps commanders, among them the disgruntled McDowell and John Fitzhugh Porter, a close associate of McClellan and thus no friend to his current superior officer, to move swiftly on Jackson, and to crush him before Lee could bring up the rest of his army in support. Early on 29 August, Pope launched his assault, but because of his subordinates' dilatoriness he only managed to get 32,000 into battle against Jackson's 22,000. The rebels made a spirited defence – resorting to throwing rocks when their ammunition ran out – and drove the Federal troops back with heavy losses. By the time Pope got round to renewing the attack the following day, the whole of Lee's army was waiting. Longstreet's corps tore through the Federal left wing, blasting great holes in its line with concentrated artillery fire: the battle was over. As was by now the established pattern, casualty rates were exceptionally high: of 65,000 Federals who fought, 16,000 fell, dead or wounded; on the rebel side, 10,000 out of a force of 55,000.

Lee now decided to seize the initiative in a bold strategic move. Washington was too heavily fortified for him to contemplate attacking it. Central and northern Virginia had been foraged over repeatedly in recent months by both sides, and could no longer supply his army with the supplies it needed. If he stayed where he was he would have to depend on a long line of supply stretching far south – impeding his freedom of movement and vulnerable to enemy attack. A less daring general would have opted for the obvious and safe course of action: withdraw southwards and dig in along one of the many rivers to await the Federals' next invasion attempt. Instead, Lee decided to invade Maryland. That autumn Federal congressional elections were due to be held; if the Confederacy could build upon their recent successes by inflicting a humiliating defeat on northern soil it could well shift the balance of seats in Congress towards anti-war Democrats. The peace faction would be further encouraged by the predictable reaction of Britain and France to a successful invasion. These countries were still toying with the idea of intervening to negotiate a settlement between the belligerents; it was public knowledge that the British Prime Minister, Lord Palmerston, was considering a pact between the major European powers to bring about peace on the basis of separation. In the west, a rebel counteroffensive under General Bragg was already underway, having scored notable successes in Tennessee and Kentucky. Now seemed a propitious moment to try to bring the war to a close.

In early September Lee's men, reinforced to 55,000, crossed the Potomac, taking with them wagon loads of stolen Federal rifles to arm the Southern sympathisers of Maryland it was anticipated would flock to the Stars and Bars. Native Marylanders, however, were content to cheer the marching columns of Confederates, awaiting the outcome of battle before committing themselves. The Army of the Potomac was now reassembled and ready to march, Lincoln having reinstated McClellan as sole commander of the forces in the east. 'Rather the devil you know,' he told his cabinet, 'than the devil you don't.' Lee's goal was the railroad junction at Harrisburg, but en route he had to deal with a twelve-thousand strong Federal garrison in Harper's Ferry, at the northern end of the Shenandoah Valley. Leaving these men at the mercy of a superior enemy force would ordinarily be considered a strategic error – they should have been withdrawn long before the rebels got near - but it inadvertently provided McClellan with a golden opportunity to crush Lee once and for all. With his cavalry acting as a screen shielding his movements, Lee divided his force, detaching part to take Harper's Ferry, while the rest headed north. McClellan in cautious pursuit – his progress impeded, as ever, by delusions about the size of the Army of Northern Virginia - was lucky enough to stumble on his adversary's campaign plans, wrapped around some cigars abandoned in a field. With quick and decisive action, Lee's army, spread out as it was, could have been destroyed piecemeal. But McClellan was not the man for the job. Eighteen hours passed before he did anything – a loss of time that critically reduced his advantage.

Aware by now that McClellan was dangerously close, Lee hastened to gather as much of his army as he could on a high ridge, west of a small creek called Antietam. At his back, lay the little town of Sharpsburg, north of which lay cornfields and orchards gathered round the church of a German pacifist sect, the Dunkers. Jackson held the left wing, around the church, a division under D.H. Hill held the centre along a sunken road, and Longstreet held the right, in front of the town. A considerable portion of Lee's army was still absent at Harper's Ferry. All day on 16 September the Union army, 75,000 strong, got into position on the other side of the Antietam.

McClellan planned to threaten Lee's right wing with the corps commanded by General Ambrose E Burnside, principally to deter Lee from transferring troops to his centre and left where the real assault was to be made. But Burnside was also instructed to turn his threatening gesture into an all out attack if circumstances proved favourable. The attack on the rebel centre and left was to be carried out by three corps (Hooker's, Mansfield's and Sumner's), while two more were held in reserve to exploit cracks in the enemy line wherever they might appear. Early next morning, Hooker's men broke from the cover of the trees that grew along the western slopes of the Antietam, and rushed across the cornfields towards Jackson's men. The rebel line reeled backed until, reinforced by troops from the centre, it in turn blasted the Federals into retreat. The next Federal corps moved up, unleashed its attack, and the opposing lines of infantry wavered to and fro as before. Sumner's corps, launching the third phase of the assault fared a little better; two divisions on its left encountered Hill's men posted in the sunken road and, finding the enemy's ranks depleted because of reinforcements sent to aid Jackson, they managed to break through. The rebel line was now, potentially, split in two. Sumner's divisions were in no condition, however, to drive home the advantage. Fortunately for Lee, McClellan dithered. He refused to commit a reserve corps to follow through, because he feared the backlash of Lee's huge reserves. After five hours, 12,000 lay dead or wounded around the little church, and three-deep in the sunken lane, and the opposing lines were in the same places they had been the day before.

Meanwhile on the Federal left, Burnside's mighty corps had been pinned down by a mere four hundred Georgians, who sniped at it from the high bluffs across the river, while rebel units hastened northwards to support their beleaguered comrades. Eventually, however, he got his men across and began pursuing the outnumbered rebels into the town. Again it looked as if McClellan had done it, for there was nothing to stop him rolling up the rebel line and sending it into a headlong rout. But the god of battles was on Lee's side that day. For the Georgians had delayed Burnside just long enough for the remainder of the Confederate army to arrive from Harper's Ferry. Footsore from a forced march of eighteen miles, the men of A P Hill's division, their commander flaunting the flaming-red shirt he always wore in battle, attacked Burnside's corps in flank and rear. McClellan refused to send in his reserves to lend support – and so Burnside's men fell back. At all points, the Federal attack had failed.

Lee's veterans had surpassed themselves, but the men with Hooker, Sumner and Mansfield had fought no less courageously. McClellan had proved an unwitting ally of the Confederates.

All next day, Lee held his men ready for the next attack. It never came. The day after, the rebels began to head south across the Potomac. The losses on 17 September far surpassed anything that had occurred before. Some rebel units reported 50% casualties. Lee's army had been reduced by nearly one third. A total of 24,000 men on both sides were killed or wounded – four times more than were to suffer on the Normandy beaches in 1944.

Despite his lamentable performance, McClellan thought himself the saviour of the nation, and proclaimed the battle of Antietam a great victory. But more procrastination followed, and the Army of the Potomac made no preparations for pursuit. Lincoln visited in person to get his general to go after the rebels. It was over a month before the army crossed the Potomac. The *Chicago Tribune* demanded to know: 'What malign influence palsies our army and wastes these glorious days for fighting? If it is McClellan, does not the President see that he his a traitor?' Lincoln, sick of trying to 'bore with an auger too dull to take hold', relieved McClellan of command, and the Army of the Potomac bade a tearful farewell to 'Little Mac'.

Bragg's Invasion Of Kentucky

In the West the Union onslaught had run out of steam. Part of the reason lay in the sheer scale of the task faced by the region's supreme commander, General Halleck. He had to organise a campaign against Vicksburg, take Chattanooga and liberate eastern Tennessee, and repair and defend hundreds of miles of rail network on which his supplies depended. Further, he had to garrison occupied territory, organise camps for 'contrabands', oversee the revival of trade and protect Unionists trying to reconstruct civil government in Tennessee. His resources, though incomparably greater than the enemy, were simply too limited for him to pursue all his objectives as swiftly as Lincoln wanted. Success, it appeared, brought its own problems.

The more rebel territory the Union army occupied, the more troops it took to hold it and to protect the ever-extending line of supply. Irregular Confederate troops, operating behind the lines, were a major headache.

Also, there were the cavalry units, like those commanded by Morgan Hunt and Nathan Bedford Forrest, which conducted wide-ranging and highly costly raids, hundreds of miles into territory ostensibly in Union possession. A restive civilian population gave both irregulars and organised rebel cavalry a great deal of support. In due course, the Union command took a tougher line, blurring the distinction between combatant and non-combatant; the civilians and property in occupied territory came to be viewed solely in terms of their potential contribution to the rebel war effort, and treated accordingly. Intransigence on the part of Southerners under occupation forced the Union army into the adoption of extreme measures, whose epitome was the scorched-earth policy implemented by General Sherman on his infamous march through Georgia.

After occupying Corinth, Halleck directed Grant to use his army (the Army of Western Tennessee) to consolidate the occupation of western Tennessee; Buell and his Army of the Ohio were to take the next key target, Chattanooga. But Buell made little progress. Impeded by rebel cavalry raids that cut his line of supply, and slowed down by the need to repair and garrison the rail connection as he moved along, he was still miles from his objective after weeks of campaigning. The initiative now passed to the Confederates.

Displeased with Beauregard's uncontested surrender of Corinth, Jefferson Davis had replaced him with one of his corps commanders, Braxton Bragg. Bragg was a strict disciplinarian, not well loved by his men, but respected for his organisational skill and his willingness to fight. Davis wanted a leader who would strike back, and Bragg seemed to fit the bill. Following the example of the rebel cavalry who had been carrying out deep strikes into Union-held territory, Bragg decided to launch his own full-scale raid. He divided his command in two: under Generals Earl Van Dorn and Stirling Price he assigned 32,000 to cover the approaches to Vicksburg, while with the remaining 34,000 he headed by a circuitous rail route for Chattanooga, arriving ahead of General Buell in late June. From there he marched north into the heart of Tennessee, co-ordinating with 18,000 troops under command of Edmund Kirby Smith, who followed a parallel route a hundred miles to the east. Bragg had instructed Van Dorn and Price to threaten Grant's army in northern Mississippi to prevent troops being sent to Buell's aid, and to commit themselves to an all-out invasion of west Tennessee should the opportunity arise. At first Bragg's plan worked well; Halleck, Grant and Buell were taken completely off guard.

By mid-August Kirby Smith had penetrated deep into Kentucky to a point 75 miles south of Cincinnati in Ohio, thus taking the war right into the backyard of the Union's Northwest. Occupying the state capitol of Frankfort, Smith set about inaugurating a Confederate state legislature. On their march north, the rebels had brought with them 15,000 rifles, hoping recruit the many thousands who were believed to be straining at the leash of Federal control. But as was the case in Maryland, the response was disappointing. The fiercely pro-Southern minority had long since fled south to enlist, while the cautious majority chose, instead, to wait and see. Buell, moving with unaccustomed speed, closed in on Bragg before he could unite with Kirby Smith. In October at Perryville, the Federal force, with a slight advantage in numbers, fought the rebels to a standstill. Having suffered heavy losses, neither side was prepared to renew the fight next day, and Bragg retreated south, with Buell in sluggish pursuit. Bragg's bold invasion was at an end.

The Emancipation Proclamation

A crucial phase of the war had ended. By November 1862 the Confederacy was once again pushed back to the line it had held six months earlier: stretching from a point about fifty miles north of Vicksburg on the Mississippi, eastwards through northern Mississippi and Alabama, into East Tennessee, key portions of which they continued to hold. In Virginia, Union and Confederate armies once again glowered at one another across the Rappahanock River, sixty miles north of Richmond. The North's congressional elections brought no landslide victory for the Democrats, and Palmerston shelved his plans for intervention.

In September Lincoln issued his Emancipation Proclamation, due to take effect 1 January 1863. The victory at Antietam had provided him with the opportunity to let people at home and abroad know that the character of the war had been transformed. The proclamation put abolition squarely at the centre of Union war aims; no longer a war between armies merely, this was now a war for the destruction of the South and the 'peculiar institution' that defined its character, and for the creation of a new Union. Though he had announced his intention to free the slaves to his cabinet the previous summer, he had thought it imprudent to issue the proclamation when the tide of war was against them. It would have smacked of desperation: a call for a slave insurrection to achieve on the home front what Union armies could not do in battle. Moreover, the indeterminate number of Northerners who were reluctant to turn the war into a fight for 'niggers' would be less likely to carp if it came from a successful administration, issuing it in the wake of a victory in the field. The proclamation diminished the chances that Britain would intervene on the side of the South, now that slavery had been turned into one of the chief issues at stake.

In a way, Lee was responsible for this transformation, for turning war from a limited one aimed at restoration of the status quo, into one for the destruction of the South. Had he not succeeded so brilliantly against McClellan outside Richmond in the spring of 1862, it is possible that a defeated South, with its 'peculiar institution' intact, would have been readmitted to the Union. Plenty of Federal army officers would have been happy with that – McClellan among them. But the Southern offensive in the summer and autumn of 1862, followed by the Emancipation Proclamation, put an end to the old Union for good.

Winter Campaigns 1862-3

Lincoln appointed a new commander for the Army of the Potomac, the man who had turned in so lacklustre a performance at Antietam: General Ambrose E Burnside. Though he looked every inch the part of the aggressive and flamboyant soldier – his carefully tended moustache and side-whiskers gave rise to a new noun, 'sideburns' -

he was to prove as dismal a failure as General Pope.

In accordance with Lincoln's directive to strike at Lee as soon as possible, in December Burnside had moved his troops to the Rappahanock River where the rebels, 75,000 in number, occupied a system of trenches and rifle pits on the hills overlooking the town of Fredericksburg. The high ground, a half a mile south of the town, was called Marye's Heights, and it was here that Longstreet's corps, with half the rebel artillery had taken up its position, as Lee's left wing. At the foot of the Heights lay a sunken road and before it a stonewall facing the side that looked towards the town. Here were posted a brigade of Alabama infantry, and immediately above them ranks of massed artillery. The ground in the intervening half-mile to the town was criss-crossed with small ravines and gullies, affording no shelter whatsoever. One rebel gunner commented: 'A chicken could not live on that field when we open up on it.' To the right of Longstreet's divisions, on a ridge continuous with the Heights, were Jackson's men.

Burnside was slow getting his men across the Rappahanock. The pontoon bridges required for the move had been unnecessarily delayed because Burnside's request for them was so vaguely worded. This allowed Lee plenty of time to prepare. Many of the engineers putting the pontoons in place fell victim to rebel sniper fire directed from Fredericksburg. This enraged the Union troops; the first units to cross stormed into the now almost abandoned town and vented their anger in an orgy of destruction. Burnside intended to launch his attack simultaneously along the entire front, determined to make the most of his advantage in numbers. On the Federal left, General Meade was to probe Jackson's line for weak points, while Sumner and Hooker were to keep Longstreet busy, holding back from outright assault until there had been a breakthrough on the left. Meade's men did well, putting enormous pressure on Jackson's men, and found a gap between the Jackson's left and Longstreet's right that, if properly exploited, could have proved fatal. But General Franklin, whose job it was to support Meade, moved so sluggishly, that the moment of opportunity passed, and Meade's corps was forced back. Over on the Federal right, meanwhile, a tentative demonstration had evolved into a full-scale assault. Along a front half a mile wide, a series of brigade-sized attacks were made against the rebels in the sunken road at the foot of the Heights, bristling with rebel ordnance. The Union troops fell like wheat before a scythe. Their dead lay neatly arranged, in the same battle formations they had advanced in. After many hours, the fighting stopped. 13,000 Union troops had fallen, most of them in front of Marye's Heights, and the rebels had not yielded one foot of ground.

Incredulous and in tears, Burnside insisted on leading another assault, with himself at the head of the line. His general staff managed to restrain him. The Union army retreated to the north side of the Rappahanock.

In the first days of the following year, Burnside tried again, moving his troops up river, hoping to flank Lee out of his trenches and force him to fight in the open. Torrential rain turned the roads into impassable swamps, and for two days the Army of the Potomac floundered in the mud. Burnside called off the campaign; within the week he had been relieved of command.

In the west that winter, the North fared indifferently. Grant planned a two-pronged approach to Vicksburg: a force under his command to move overland, east of the Mississippi, while a separate force, under Sherman, moved down river with the aid of Porter's flotilla of gunboats. The rebels assigned to protect Vicksburg were now preparing for a siege. In trying to support Bragg's invasion, by advancing on Federal positions in west Tennessee, Van Dorn and Price had been roughly handled by Union troops under the command of General Rosecrans. General Pemberton, assigned to take over from them, had withdrawn Confederate troops to the vicinity of Vicksburg; an officer with a special knowledge of artillery and fortification, he had begun constructing a formidable system of trenches and gun emplacements. Sherman made good progress and, disembarking above the town on the east bank of the river, got ready to attack. Unfortunately, Grant was nowhere in sight. Confederate General Nathan Bedford Forrest had led a few thousand cavalry on one of his spectacular raids around enemy lines, burning and looting, tearing up mile on mile of track, and had forced Grant's half of the expedition to come to a halt. But because Forrest had also destroyed the telegraph lines, Grant was unable to alert Sherman. The 30,000 Union troops who attacked the entrenched rebels outside the town were easily repulsed, with considerable loss.

In the remainder of the winter and well into the spring, Grant was to make repeated attempts to get his armies into position to take Vicksburg – all of them failures.

While Federal troops in the Mississippi Valley suffered a setback, their colleagues further east under Rosecrans had better luck. After his success against Van Dorn and Price, Rosecrans was given Buell's army and told to attack Bragg at once – which he proceeded to do. In a battle lasting two days, fought at the turn of the year at Stones' River, both sides suffered nearly 30% casualties. Yet neither side won any tactical advantage over its opponent. But it was Bragg, who, after initially telegraphing Davis with news of his victory, decided to pull back when the Union retreat he had anticipated failed to materialise. The rebels now concentrated around Chattanooga, in the far south of Tennessee.

The High Tide Of War, Spring And Autumn 1863

Fall Of Vicksburg

In the winter of 1862-3 Northern newspapers were full of rumours about Grant: chiefly, that his failure to take Vicksburg was the result of a resurgence of the heavy drinking that had blighted his pre-war army career. Lincoln sent Charles A Dana, a member of the War Department, to see if it was true. So impressed was he with Grant that he became one of his most loyal supporters. Grant, wrote Dana, was 'the most modest, most disinterested and most honest man I ever knew, with a temper nothing could disturb…. Not a great man except morally; not an original or brilliant man, but sincere, thoughtful, deep and gifted with courage that never faltered.' There may have been some truth in the rumours, however. Throughout his life Grant depended on his wife, Julia, to keep his alcoholism under control: during the war, that role passed to his chief of staff, John Rawlins. He was most likely to succumb during periods of frustration and inactivity, and it was just such a phase that his Vicksburg campaign had entered. But by a bold and characteristic move, which Sherman considered insane, Grant solved his strategic problem.

Time and again, the Federal invasion of the west had been impeded by its reliance on long lines of supply, which presented vulnerable targets to enemy cavalry while decreasing the combat strength of armies in the field. Grant decided on a radical plan; he would abandon his line of supply and live off the land. It was true that the local civilian population were suffering a great deal of hardship as a result of food shortages, but he rightly surmised that this was due to the hoarding of crops on the part of farmers. Soldiers would be able to take by force what the worthless currency of local civilians was unable to buy. He planned to take the bulk of his army down the west bank of the Mississippi, supported by Porter's gunboats, cross south of Vicksburg to its east bank, and march on it from the south. This was successfully carried out with the assistance of two diversionary forays; a force under Sherman feigned a landing north of the town, while a former infantry officer with an aversion to horses, General Grierson, carried out a spectacular cavalry raid deep into enemy territory.

For the first eighteen months of the war, it was generally acknowledged on both sides that rebel cavalry could outfight and outride its Union counterpart. Grierson's raid showed that was no longer true. With only 1,700 men he severely disrupted Pemberton's supply line, burning stores and ripping up miles of irreplaceable railway track, luring away in futile pursuit an entire division of rebel infantry. In just over two weeks he and his men rode four hundred miles, killed a hundred rebels and took a further five hundred prisoner. Forrest, Morgan and Stuart at last had a rival.

Grant had two rebel forces to contend with: 30,000 under Pemberton, in and around Vicksburg; 6,000 (but growing all the time) under J E Johnston at Jackson, the state capital, some sixty miles east of Vicksburg. Before dealing with Pemberton, he needed to neutralise the threat from Johnston, to prevent an assault on his rear while he was moving against his main target. Fortunately he was able to count on the inept and divided counsel of the rebel high command. Johnston favoured uniting the two forces, luring Grant onto ground of his own choice and destroying him. In overall command of rebel forces in the west, Johnston should have had his way but Pemberton refused to move far from Vicksburg. Davis had instructed him to hold the town at all costs, and hold it he would. So Grant was able to deal with the rebel armies piecemeal, which, if combined, would have almost matched his own in numbers. Moving swiftly towards Jackson, Grant drove off Johnston and took possession of the town. Turning west with the bulk of his army to confront and overwhelm a force under Pemberton at Champion's Hill, he left Sherman with his corps to finish things off in the state capital. Jackson got a foretaste of what was in store for the Deep South the following year when Sherman made his notorious 'March to the Sea'; 'Chimneyville' is how Sherman's men referred to Jackson after they had finished with it.

Advancing from Champion's Hill, Grant encountered feeble rebel resistance at a river, the Big Black, some miles east of his goal. Roughly handled, Pemberton hastily withdrew behind his ring of rifle-pits and trenches, many miles long, around Vicksburg. In a magnificent 17-day campaign, Grant had marched his men over 180 miles, fought and won five separate engagements, and inflicted over 7,000 casualties; and he now appeared to be on the brink of seizing the objective towards which the Union armies had been working their way for over eight months. Though Vicksburg's defences were formidable, Grant felt it was worth the risk of an immediate assault; in any case, after a string of successes, his men were in no mood to dig-in and starve the rebels into submission. Reinforced to 70,000 by newly recruited units, Grant's army unleashed bloody but fruitless assaults over the course of two days. On 21 May, the Union army relented, entrenching for what was to be a six-week siege. During this time, Grant's only worry – and Pemberton's only hope – was that Johnston, with a force now numbering 30,000 and hovering somewhere off to the northeast, would smash through the encircling Union army from the rear and relieve the town. But neither Johnston nor his army – it consisted mostly of raw recruits – were up to the task. By the end of June conditions in the town were appalling. Reduced to eating dogs, cats and even rats, living in caves they had cut out of the bluffs above the river to avoid the incessant artillery bombardment (many were driven mad by the strain), civilians and soldiers pleaded with Pemberton to surrender. On 4 July 1863, Grant's army entered the town. 'The father of waters,' said Lincoln when he heard the news of the victory, 'goes unvexed to the sea.' It was a turning point in the war: the Confederacy was split in half, ready to be cut up into small portions and subjugated.

Chancellorsville: Lee's Finest Hour

The Union war effort in the east had ground to a halt in the mud. Lincoln tried to put new heart into the Army of the Potomac by installing 'Fighting' Joe Hooker as its new commander. Hard-drinking, profane and pugnacious, Hooker was also proud, boastful and somewhat disloyal; angling for his commander's job, he had been free with caustic comments about the quality of Burnside's leadership. Now he was to get his chance. Mindful of the serious task ahead of him, Hooker stopped drinking, and set about restoring his men's morale, in which task he succeeded admirably. The Army of the Potomac was soon on its feet again and ready to have another crack at heading south to Richmond. New units arriving daily, it now numbered 120,000.

Along a twenty-five mile stretch, Lee still occupied the high ground overlooking Fredericksburg on the Rappahanock – an impregnable position his 40,000 could easily defend against an army more than twice their size. Lee's numbers had been reduced by two divisions being detailed for duty under Longstreet in the Carolinas, gathering forage and food, and working on coastal defences. Hooker planned a bold manoeuvre. Distracting Lee with a feint towards the front of his position, he would send the bulk of his army sweeping around the rebel left flank and rear. It was well planned and executed. The Union cavalry outdid itself, successfully concealing the flanking movement, and carrying out a dashing and destructive raid on Lee's lines of communication. Stuart's cavalry, lured off in pursuit, was slow to detect the massive concentration of troops – 70,000 – that was taking place on Lee's left. By the night of 30 April, five Union corps had assembled at a small hamlet called Chancellorsville. If

Hooker moved swiftly the next day, Lee would be forced, he hoped, into headlong retreat.

The terrain south of the river was covered in a thick tangle of forest and undergrowth, known locally as 'the Wilderness'. Visibility was restricted to a few hundred yards at best, and movement was possible only along a handful of narrow and winding dirt roads. Such conditions could easily destroy the advantage of superior numbers; the range of the artillery would be severely restricted; gaps in the enemy line would go undetected and, thus, unexploited. 'The Wilderness' would do much, if Hooker was not careful, to even the odds between the two sides.

When the news reached him, Lee decided to make a fight of it. Leaving a small force in the trenches to face the Federal troops before Fredericksburg, he led the remainder, though heavily outnumbered, to attack the enemy at Chancellorsville. From the first, Hooker lost the advantage; though occupying clear ground over which his greater numbers and artillery would be most effective, he withdrew west to a position more easily defended within the confusion of scrub oak and thorny undergrowth. Having started out off with a highly successful piece of aggressive strategy, Hooker unaccountably decided to go on the defensive. His own corps commanders were furious. Why had they launched the campaign, if it was not to smash Lee's army in an attack committing the full weight of their numbers? That day, the lines wavered back and forth in 'the Wilderness', with little ground gained or lost on either side. But Lee had made an important discovery; 'Fighting' Joe had no stomach for the battle he had brought on.

During the next two days of fighting, Hooker reacted as if in a daze. Once his miraculous flanking manoeuvre had failed to scare Lee into retreating he seems to have run out of ideas. He kept on looking for signs of a rebel withdrawal, and when they failed to appear, he was stumped, incapable of framing an aggressive response. Maybe he shouldn't have gone on the wagon; a drop or two might have supplied him with just the fighting spirit he now so obviously lacked.

Lee's counter-stoke was masterly and audacious. During the night, he sent Jackson with 30,000 troops on a wide flanking march around Hooker's right, while he held the position in front of Hooker with a mere 10,000. For a time, Lee's army was divided into three parts, any one of which could have been destroyed by the enemy in its vicinity. Jackson, in column formation stretching many miles, was especially vulnerable. But Lee was gambling on the cowed mentality of his opponent, and on 'the Wilderness' concealing his movements from an enemy inclined to sit tight behind its defences. Of all his battles, Chancellorsville is the one most highly esteemed by military analysts. When Jackson struck the rear and flank of the Federal right late on the afternoon of 2 May, he pushed it back several miles before supporting corps from elsewhere in the line could come to its aid.

The fighting dragged on the next day, with Hooker reforming on a still stronger defensive position, both flanks anchored on the river. It is further evidence of Hooker's defeated mentality that, though early on in the fight Lee had committed the entirety of his command to battle, holding nothing back, Hooker, on the other hand, continued to hold two corps in reserve. Events at the other end of the battle seemed to offer him a chance. His left wing drove the rebels from their trenches above Fredericksburg and began to threaten Lee's rear. But to make anything of this, Hooker would have had to be ready to attack Lee's newly formed line in his front; and this he was not willing to do. So when Lee turned to confront the Federal forces en route from the town, they were stopped in their tracks.

On 4 May, after losing 15% of his force in killed and wounded, Hooker withdrew to the north bank of the Rappahanock. The Army of the Potomac had been once again bludgeoned to a standstill. Lee had lost 13,000 and, his most serious loss of the war, General Jackson, who was killed accidentally by his own men while returning from night reconnaissance during the battle.

Lee's Second Invasion Of The North

In the wake of his staggering success at Chancellorsville, Lee saw an opportunity of ending the war. In the west, Grant was currently embroiled in a prolonged siege outside Vicksburg. Johnston was building up his strength to relieve it. Bragg, despite withdrawing from Stones' River, still held on in lower east Tennessee. The Army of the Potomac had just suffered its most humiliating defeat of the war. The scales of victory were once again in equipoise, and vigorous action on the Confederacy's part might tip them in its favour. If Lee carried the war onto Northern soil, as he had done the previous autumn, he would bolster the Northern peace party, and encourage European governments to reconsider recognition. Indeed a pro-Southern faction was still active in Britain, and in June a Member of Parliament spoke in favour of joint intervention by Her Majesty's Government and Napoleon III.

Moreover, there was once again the issue of supplies. Virginia had been fought and foraged over continually since the outbreak of war, and the blockade, effective for more than a year, was choking off all imports. If it were to keep going, the Army of Northern Virginia simply had to get supplies from somewhere - and where better than the rich farms of Maryland and Pennsylvania? There were those in the Confederate high command who argued for the priority of relieving Vicksburg, suggesting that while Lee watched the beaten Hooker with a fraction of his army, Longstreet should take the rest to Johnston and help deliver a knockout blow to Grant. But in the euphoria emanating from Chancellorsville, Davis was in no mind to deny Lee anything.

Why was Lee so adamant that the winning campaign should take place in the east? If rebel armies had combined to defeat Grant and relieve Vicksburg, in addition to maintaining the Confederacy intact, this would have bolstered the Northern peace party just as effectively, and encouraged Britain and France to recognise Southern independence. The problem of supplies for the Army of Northern Virginia would have been solved, at least to some degree, by reducing the numbers that local resources had to cater for. Though never criticised for his tactical ability and the quality of his leadership, it is sometimes suggested that Lee suffered from a narrowness of outlook in his overview of the war, and his insistence on invading in the east in 1863 cited as an example. Lee, it is claimed, simply ignored the war outside Virginia. Moreover, he betrayed a desire to hog the limelight, wanting all the decisive actions to be executed by his own Army of Northern Virginia. He was blinded by his determination to punish the enemy – 'those people' as he called the Union army – for daring to invade his 'country', Virginia. However, it can be argued that Lee's lack of interest in the western theatre proceeded from an accurate assessment of where the war was to be won. The Confederacy could at best fail to lose the war in the Mississippi River Valley; the strategy best suited here was one of dogged defence at minimal cost, yielding ground as necessary in order to gain time. The Union Northwest lacked any significant targets for a rebel invasion force. Further, as Lee appreciated, the quality of the Confederacy's western command was poor. Whereas, in Virginia there was a real prospect of victory, through so mauling and humiliating the Army of the Potomac that both domestic and foreign pressure brought about a ceasefire. And in Lee and the Army of Northern Virginia, the Confederacy possessed exactly wanted it needed to achieve the requisite victories.

The army that marched northwards in June was in much better shape than when it invaded the previous autumn. After resting and refitting for a month, and with the return of Longstreet and his men, the Army of Northern Virginia was in fine fettle – 75,000 strong, exhilarated by its victory of the previous month, and eager to wage war on enemy soil for a change. Following Jackson's death, Lee reorganised his army into three corps, commanded by Generals Ewell, Longstreet and A P Hill. By the last week of June his army was in the north of the Valley, en route for Williamsburg, state capital of Pennsylvania. Alerted to their movements by his scouts, Hooker, still evincing a reluctance to come to grips with his enemy, proposed to Lincoln that he ignore the rebels and, instead, march south to Richmond. Lincoln responded by replacing him with one of his corps commanders, George G Meade.

Though a proficient and courageous commander, much respected by his men, Meade was an unknown quantity to the rest of the army. But by now, after so long and so disastrous a sequence of commanding generals, the Army of the Potomac had ceased to care. In previous battles, the mettle of the common fighting soldier and of the middle-ranking officers – and even some division and corps commanders – had been proved every bit as good as that of Lee's troops. There was nothing wrong with the pluck and fighting capacity of the army; the fault lay in the calibre of the generals picked to lead it. There was a feeling abroad that, no matter who led them, no matter how it turned out, the men would continue to fight. This determination was fed in the coming campaign by something new. For the first time, the men of the Army of the Potomac were going to be fighting on their home ground and, as it were, before an audience of their family and friends. (The conditions under which they fought at Antietam had not been quite the same, for though a part of the Union, Maryland was, by its nature, a Southern state.) They were to have an advantage customarily enjoyed by Lee's men.

Quite soon, Lee's plans began to miscarry. Stuart, his high spirited and daring cavalry commander, had been outsmarted and roughly handled by the Union cavalry at Chancellorsville. Determined to recover face, he set off on a far-ranging and highly destructive raid around the Union army. Consequently, until the end of the second day of Gettysburg, Lee was without the bulk of his cavalry. Without 'his eyes' Lee had no idea of the enemy's movements. As a result, he was forced into a fight on ground that he had not chosen, and spent the first two days of battle launching attacks against an enemy whose dispositions and strengths he could only guess. If there is one cause of defeat all commentators agree on, it is the absence of Stuart in the critical days at the end of June.

The battle was precipitated by a hunt for shoes. On 1 July, heading for Gettysburg, where he had heard of a big supply of this badly needed item,

71

A P Hill encountered stiff resistance northwest of the town from two brigades of dismounted Union cavalry. Though he deployed most of a division of infantry, they managed to hold him back until a Union corps under Reynolds arrived on the scene. Soon a further Union corps joined the fray. Hastily getting into line, they opened fire on a further Confederate force which appeared north of the town – the divisions formerly commanded by Jackson and now led by a veteran of the Valley Campaign, Richard S Ewell. Two Union and two Confederate infantry corps were now involved in the fighting. From morning through into late afternoon, on a curved front stretching round the north and west of Gettysburg, the ranks of blue and grey poured volley and counter-volley into each other's ranks. Eventually, the Union right flank began to crumble, and soon the whole line was pulling back to high ground southeast of the town. But they had done a good job, holding back the rebels until the rest of the Union army could arrive and prepare a defensive position.

Southeast of Gettysburg was a line of elevated ground called Cemetery Ridge, running roughly north-south. At its northern end were a couple of hills – Culp's and Cemetery – which curved round so as to form a hook. At the southern end was another pair of hills, called Little Round Top and Big Round Top. The whole formed a natural line of defence, whose convexity allowed the swift transfer of troops from one sector to another while providing the Union commander an overview of his entire position – both of which advantages it denied Lee. The outward curve of the rebel line forced him to fight with little knowledge of what was happening on his left wing. This was to prove disastrous. But towards the end of the first day, Lee still had a chance to roll up the Union line before it got properly settled in. If his left moved rapidly and with sufficient determination, it could take Cemetery and Culp's Hills, bear down on the Union flank and rout the enemy. But that part of Lee's line was in the hands of Ewell, and, throughout the battle, Ewell displayed a marked absence of his predecessor's zeal. Lee, mistaking his man, requested, rather than ordered, Ewell to probe the Union position on the hills, with a view to developing a full-scale assault. Ewell made a half-hearted advance, and then fell back. Jackson would have swept all before him. If that part of his line had been in properly in view, there is no doubt that Lee would have insisted on the attack being vigorously driven home.

Next morning Meade's army was ranged along the ridge and around the hills at the northern end, a force 90,000 strong. Since the burden of the first day's fighting had fallen to Ewell and A P Hill, Lee assigned the attack on the second day to Longstreet, whose men had arrived during the course of the night. But Longstreet was not pleased with the way things were going. The Federals held a strong position and, though precise figures were unavailable, they clearly outnumbered the Confederates. Lee was proposing an attack across open ground against troops protected by breastworks and amply supported with artillery – the comparison with Marye's Heights at Fredericksburg was surely obvious. Might it not be better, Longstreet queried, to flank Meade's left, oust him from his high ground and force him to fight somewhere a little less inequitable, and of Lee's own choosing? But Lee would hear none of this. His men had already pitched into the enemy and sent them flying. He had come to deliver a knockout blow; the fight had started and he was not about to postpone it, possibly damaging his men's fighting edge in the process.

In the years after the war, Southerners made a scapegoat of Longstreet. After being rebuffed by Lee, they said, he went into a sulk, and though charged with the burden of the fighting on the second and third days, carried out orders in so sluggish manner as to virtually sabotage the Confederates. Besides, of all Lee's senior commanders, Longstreet, they added, was the only one not from Virginia – no wonder he failed 'Marse Robert' at the critical moment! But Lee has his critics too. Meade's position was well chosen and fortified, and it might have been better to seek a battle in which the rebels, being in the minority, could play the defensive role. Lee, driven by a determination to get the job done, and still heady, as were his men, with Chancellorsville euphoria, simply would not listen to the cooler and more reasonable counsel of his lieutenant. Longstreet of course had not shared in the glory of two months before, and so did not experience the, possibly, deluding effects of that euphoria.

Lee instructed Longstreet to break the Federal left. Ewell was ordered to take the hills he had found too heavily defended to approach the previous day – a task he undertook with same lack of spirit, and success, as before. Longstreeet, with two of his three divisions and the one division of A P Hill that had not fought the previous day, after many hours of delay, occasioned by the need to stay out of sight of a Federal observation post on one of the Round Tops, launched the attack in mid-afternoon. The corps he was attacking had, in fact, been pushed far in advance of the rest of the Union line, and its flank could easily have been turned. General Sickles, commanding this sector of the line, had moved it to a road that ran southwards from the town, and into a peach orchard and a stretch of rocky ground known as Devil's Den, at the foot of the Round Tops, which were themselves unoccupied. The Union left, far from being anchored in those hills, as Meade intended, was left floating. But it is a measure of Longstreet's disaffection that he failed to make anything of this opportunity. To do so would have meant adjusting his objectives, and after being rebuffed so forcefully by his chief, he was now reluctant to approach Lee with a further proposed revision to his plan. None of this, however, prevented his troops from giving Sickles' men a severe thumping. Driving them back from the road, they forced them up on to the line it was intended by Meade they occupy in the first place. Some of the Confederate regiments did, as it happened, try to seize the Round Tops when it was clear that they were empty. In the nick of time, a Union regiment, the twentieth Maine, was rushed into position, managing to get to the summit of Little Round Top, minutes before a brigade of Alabamians. Though losing more than half their number in the space of forty minutes, they stood their ground. Fighting on until their ammunition ran out, they resorted to a bayonet charge. The rebels fell back in confusion, many so astonished that they threw down their weapons and surrendered. As dusk fell, the rest of Longstreet's troops withdrew.

On the third day, Lee intended to pierce the centre of the enemy line, which he believed must now be in a weakened state, due to troops having been shifted to the flanks to deal with the previous day's assaults. Longstreet was to lead the attack on the centre, while Ewell was to try again on the Union right, the two linking up in the rear of the enemy line. But Ewell fared no better than before and was out of the running by midmorning, having pushed his assault with by now accustomed faint-heartedness. This left the brunt of that day's work to Longstreet.

At one o'clock, 150 Confederate guns opened fire on the Federal line. For two hours, until their ammunition began to run out, the rebel gunners kept pounding the enemy with shot and shell in preparation for the infantry assault that was to follow. At first Union gunners returned their fire, creating an ear-splitting roar that was heard for miles around. But after a while, the Union artillery fell silent, determined to have a sufficient reserve to face what they knew was about to come. Despite the vast expenditure of lead, the rebel batteries did little damage; most of the Federal infantry escaped injury, lying down out of harm's way on the reverse side of the ridge.

At three o'clock, the eleven brigades assigned for the assault got into line, and along a mile-long front 15,000 grey-clad soldiers began to advance. They had to cover three-quarters of a mile before they could get to grips with the enemy; the intervening ground was without cover, the afternoon was fair and bright. Leading the line was General George Pickett and his division; on rearguard duty until that morning, they had not yet fought in the battle. A flamboyant character, Pickett wore his hair in long ringlets and professed a passion for the cut and thrust of battle – though he had, in fact, seen little significant action since his enlistment. The Federal artillery opened up, blasting great holes in the grey lines. Most of the Federal infantry held their fire until the rebels got to within two hundred yards. The Union regiments that overlapped the ends of Pickett's line swept forward and fired into the flanks of those who had managed to get this far. Despite the storm of steel opposing them, some two hundred Tennesseeans and Virginians broke through the enemy breastworks, only to be cut down by further volleys that greeted them on the other side. All that survived were taken prisoner. In less then half an hour it was all over. Half the men who followed Pickett lay dead or wounded; his division had lost more than two thirds of its number.

Though mortified by his losses, and begging forgiveness of the bedraggled survivors as they stumbled back, Lee quickly recovered himself and prepared for a Union counterattack. But Meade and his generals seemed paralysed by their success. They had shattered the myth of the enemy's invincibility that had dogged them for years. Meade may well have missed a golden opportunity to destroy the Army of Northern Virginia. Lee had lost a third of his force and could muster fewer than 50,000 combatants, while Meade, who had from the first outnumbered him, had suffered fewer casualties and still had a reserve of 20,000 men. But it is understandable that Meade should have let his adversary retreat unmolested. He had been in command of the army less than a week when this torrential bloodbath occurred, and was still finding his feet. And he was naturally apprehensive about turning a stunning victory into defeat through an ill-advised assault. So Lee's men were allowed to limp away, back down the Valley.

The first week of July 1863 was the turning point of the war. With the fall of Vicksburg the Confederacy was split in two, and Lee's army would never again carry war onto Northern soil, or triumph so brilliantly over the enemy as he had done in the first two years of the fighting.

The Rebels On The Run
Winter 1863 To April 1865

The West: Chickamauga And Chattanooga

In the west, the autumn and winter of 1863 saw the repetition of the pattern by now well established: the faltering but seemingly inexorable advance of Union armies in face of a steadily retreating enemy. The Confederate armies continued to suffer from a lack of direction at the top, and from being divided into two forces, that of Johnston and Bragg. Only by concentrating its forces in the prosecution of a single overarching plan, under the determined leadership of one man, was there any hope for the Confederacy in the west but this proved impossible to attain.

Through a series of brilliant and bloodless manoeuvres, Rosecrans managed to push Bragg almost out of Tennessee. When the latter withdrew to Chattanooga near the state's southern border, further skilful moves on the Federal general's part forced Bragg to abandon the town. Chattanooga had been one of the key strategic goals for the Union; it lay at the junction of the South's last surviving railway network, and was a natural jumping-off point for a move against Atlanta – and from there, the heart of the Confederacy was wide open to attack. Though he had accomplished much, and at little cost in human life, Rosecrans did not command the unqualified admiration of Lincoln. He had moved too slowly, and his failure to keep up the pressure on Bragg earlier in the year had allowed several rebel divisions to be diverted to the armies in Mississippi struggling to save Vicksburg. Rosecrans, for his part, felt keenly Lincoln's lack of gratitude. The president, he felt, would have rated his accomplishments more highly had they been written in letters of blood.

But the Federals were about to get a surprise. The battle that nearly derailed the Union war effort, and that curtailed Rosecrans' career, is known by the name of 'Chickamauga' (said to mean 'river of blood'): more men were killed or wounded here than in any other battle in the western theatre. Davis thought it was time that Bragg stopped retreating and hit back instead. He reinforced him with troops taken from elsewhere (among them Longstreet and his corps) to give him roughly the same number as Rosecrans. In a battle fought over two days, involving a frontal assault on the whole of the Federal line, Bragg came close to annihilating the enemy – thanks chiefly to a quarter mile gap in the Union position, the result of a mistake in its battle orders, into which Longstreet's men charged. Rosecrans' right wing turned and ran back to Chattanooga; his headquarters caught in the wake of the rout, he was swept along with it. But one of his corps commanders, George Thomas, held firm with the rest of the army, permitting an orderly retreat to Chattanooga – an achievement that earned him the soubriquet 'the Rock of Chickamauga'.

After his victory, nothing went right for Bragg. The dissension that had intermittently undermined his army's efforts ever since he had been in command broke out again. He accused some of his senior officers of poorly executing their orders in the battle and had one of his corps commanders arrested. They, in turn, were loud in their criticisms of his leadership, and called on Davis to relieve him, which Davis, for want of anyone better, could not bring himself to do. Bragg seemed overwhelmed by the scale of his own losses – 20,000 killed or wounded, a third of his force – and refused to authorise the rapid pursuit his corps commanders insisted on. Forrest, who had joined Bragg for what he expected would be the first blow in a campaign to recover Tennessee, was disgusted with his senior's inactivity. 'What does he fight battles for?' he demanded petulantly, and promptly left for an independent command in Mississippi.

For a month or more the Federal army had the unusual experience of being besieged. Bragg's army surrounded the town and cut off supplies. Federal pack mules, and even cavalry horses were slaughtered for food; every fence and wooden shack in the town was torn apart for fuel. It was now November, and winter was setting in.

But the return match was not long in coming. Lincoln put Grant in sole charge of affairs in the west and the new commander in chief moved swiftly into action. He replaced Rosecrans with Thomas as head of the Army of the Cumberland, broke the rebel stranglehold on the town, and built up Union troops in the area to 72,000, in readiness for his counterattack. But while his enemy's strength was increasing, Bragg saw his own diminish. In yet another foolish piece of meddling, Davis decided that the key town of Knoxville in East Tennessee, recently fallen to Union forces under Burnside, had to be retaken, and he sent Longstreet with 12,000 men to do it. This expedition came to nothing, merely serving to deprive Bragg of troops he was about to need.

The rebels occupied hilly ground to the east (called Missionary Ridge) and Look Out Mountain to the south, from which they had for several weeks been lobbing shells into the town. Grant's first move was to take the mountain, and this job he assigned to Hooker. With units transferred from the Army of the Potomac, Hooker proceeded to undo some of the harm inflicted on his reputation at Chancellorsville. Losing less than 500 men, he took the mountain, driving the rebels back to their comrades on Missionary Ridge. During the battle, fog had gathered around the troops as they fought at high altitude, and this gave rise to the name, 'the battle above the clouds'.

This phase accomplished, there was a brief lull. Photographers appeared on the peaks, and Hooker with some of his officers stopped for a photo opportunity.

The rebels on Missionary Ridge were well protected by breastworks, rifle-pits and plenty of artillery. Though considerably outnumbered, the Confederates had every reason to believe they could win. Grant intended to overwhelm Bragg by launching simultaneous attacks into both his wings, while threatening his centre with that portion of his force made up of the Army of the Cumberland, Rosecrans' old army. Having had such rough treatment at Chickamauga, these men, it was assumed, would be too demoralised to perform any more demanding role. The attacks on Bragg's wings ran into trouble. So Grant ordered Thomas to bring more pressure to bear on the centre. Along a two-mile front, the twenty-three thousand men of the Army of the Cumberland swept forward. They reached their target, but, instead of regrouping and staying put as ordered, kept on going. With shouts of 'Remember Chickamauga' they pushed up to the ridge, using the dips and swells of the ground to shelter from rebel rifle fire, and took first one, then another of the line of rifle pits. The rebels fell back, failed to rally, and fled in headlong retreat. Meanwhile, Grant and Thomas watched through field glasses, incredulous, as the Army of the Cumberland stood their battle plan on its head, and won a resounding victory.

Bragg managed to get enough of his troops organised to cover the rebels' retreat. Strong resistance dissuaded Grant from vigorous pursuit. But enough had been accomplished, and the way to Atlanta was open.

Grant Takes Command

After receiving news of the fall of Vicksburg, Lincoln is reported to have said: 'Grant is my man and I am his for the rest of the war.' Federal success at Chattanooga confirmed Lincoln in this resolve, and in the spring of 1864 he appointed Grant supreme commander of the Union armies. Moving east, Grant made his headquarters with the Army of the Potomac, deciding to accompany it in what he expected to be the last phase of its efforts to smash Lee's army and capture Richmond. He instructed Meade: 'Lee's army will be your objective. Wherever Lee goes, there you will also go.' In the west he made Sherman his replacement, confident that his friend and erstwhile comrade in arms would not spare himself or his men in pursuit of the goals he now set him: 'to move against Johnston's army, to break it up, and to get into the interior of the enemy's country as far as you can, inflicting all the damage you can against their war resources.' Both the armies in the east and in the west were to maintain the pressure on their opposing forces simultaneously so as to prevent the movement of troops from quiet sectors to others currently under pressure. And a more ruthless policy was to be implemented against the civilian population and its property in portions of the Confederacy under occupation.

As the Union armies pushed their way into ever-larger tracts of the former Confederacy, the troops left behind to protect the lines of supply and to man the garrisons became embroiled in guerrilla warfare. In addition to the devastating cavalry raids conducted by the likes of Forrest, Morgan and Wheeler, they had to contend with the permanent though elusive presence of irregulars, bands of between 50 and 500 in number, who, operating in outlaw style, would attack and destroy vulnerable targets of opportunity, disappearing as rapidly as they had emerged. Such groups had the support of an indeterminable number of local farmers and townspeople, among them people who had retaken the oath of allegiance and were ostensibly loyal to the Union. The cost to the Federals exacted by this war behind their own lines was considerable – not least in the number of troops held back from frontline duty. Half of Sherman's army when it was investing Atlanta was not available for combat service against the rebels because of the need to protect his supply line from attack.

In this way the overwhelming advantage in numbers enjoyed by the North was to a considerable degree mitigated. Indeed, though the winter of '63-64 saw the rebels in retreat from Chattanooga, and on the defensive on the south bank of the Rappahanock, deep in Virginia, there were still reasons for hope in the South. The chief of these was the North's forthcoming presidential election. Lincoln's first term of office was due to expire in November, and, as is customary in the US, campaigning would be getting under way the previous spring.

Factions in the north hostile to the war were still active. The Democrats were vocal in their criticism of Lincoln's conduct of the war. The chief bones of contention were the violation of civil rights involved in implementing conscription (which began on a small scale in early 1863), the introduction of an income tax to pay for the war, the role of emancipation (mobs were still apt to turn ugly when told that their loved ones were falling in battle for the sake of 'a bunch of damn niggers') and, not least, the sheer volume of the killing. Many questioned the wisdom of persisting in the attempt to restore the Union by coercion: was it not time, they asked, to call an armistice and try settling their differences peacefully? There is little agreement among historians on the extent of this disaffection with the war, but it is certain that it played a large role in the calculations of Davis and his generals. 'If we can break up the enemy's arrangements early,' wrote Longstreet, 'and throw him back, he will not be able to recover his position or his morale until the presidential election is over, and then we shall have a new president to treat with.' This was the key to Confederate strategy in the approaching year. If the rebels could simply hold out, exacting terrible punishment for every Union gain, then the Northern electorate might reject Lincoln in favour of a Peace Democrat. The former commander of the Army of the Potomac, George McClellan, was the opposition candidate, and known to favour an armistice. That the Confederates were still intent on secession was not necessarily a problem; once the fighting stopped it would prove very hard to get it started again, especially if Britain and France were invited to participate in negotiations.

There was a further factor that might assist the South. Despite Lincoln's endorsement of conscription he was reluctant to make full use of it; rather than coerce men into his armies he preferred to get them voluntarily. In the coming year the term of enlistment was due to expire for those who had signed on for a three-year period; they numbered many hundreds of thousands. Lincoln would not use conscription to make them fight on. But Confederate victories might discourage them from volunteering to re-enlist, thus substantially reducing the Union's armies. And even if troops recruited from the North's seemingly inexhaustible civilian population were to offset these losses, yet it would still be to the South's advantage that raw recruits would be taking the places of battled-hardened veterans. In the event, 100,000 Federal troops whose term expired in the first half of 1864 failed to re-enlist, which undoubtedly, though incalculably, assisted the rebel war effort.

Grant's Offensive In Virginia, Spring And Summer 1864

The eleven months of fighting that began that spring in Virginia was unlike anything that had gone before. Most of the previous engagements had taken place between units manoeuvring largely in the open, using breastworks and entrenchments for restricted areas of their line. The fighting had lasted for no longer than three or four days, in most cases, no more than a day. What now took place between the opposing armies was very different. Through a six-week cycle of marching, entrenching and fighting, Union and Confederate troops fought continually. And at the end of it, in June, outside the town of Petersburg a few miles south of Richmond, the two armies built mile upon mile of opposed systems of trenches, in which they were to sit fighting it out, again with no letup, for a further eight months.

At the start of May, Grant moved his army of 115,000 southwards across the Rapidan, a tributary of the Rappahanock. It was the first of a series of flanking manoeuvres that were to be the hallmark of the campaign. Grant would move around Lee's right flank in an effort to draw him out into open battle, while 'the wily grey fox' (as Lee was known) would anticipate his adversary, racing ahead of him to a fortify a new position, out of which Grant would manoeuvre him once again.

It is worth noting that the extremely high losses in the ensuing months were as much Lee's responsibility as Grant's. Northern newspapers dubbed Grant, 'the Butcher', when the casualty lists began appearing and posterity has been inclined to endorse this view. Lee, by contrast, historians tend to exonerate. But Grant's aim was to draw Lee out into a major battle in which the matter could be settled once and for all. Understandably, 'the wily grey fox', with an army nearly half the size of Grant's, refused to be drawn. It was Lee who turned it into a campaign of attrition, entrenching his entire force at every opportunity. In this way, because attacks on his trench systems cost the enemy twice the number of his own casualties, he managed to neutralise the effect of being severely outnumbered – for a time at least. Eventually, the enormous disparity in manpower reserves began to tell. Though the rate of loss on the Confederate side was lower, the killed and wounded simply could not be replaced, whereas, however reluctantly at times, new recruits for the Army of the Potomac just kept on coming.

The first clash occurred in 'the Wilderness', scene of so much misery for the Union troops in the previous spring. Both flanks of Grant's army came under attack, but, despite heavy losses, refused to break. His men, used to their commanders giving up after the first serious bloodletting, expected to be withdrawn, and were jubilant on discovering, instead, that their new general intended to keep moving forward. At the little hamlet of Spotsylvania, to the south, the blue and the grey fought again; then again, at the North Anna River; at Topotomy creek; and, in mid-June, outside Cold Harbour. Here Grant ordered a murderous and fruitless assault in which 7,000 fell in less than an hour – it was the only military decision, he wrote in his memoirs, he ever regretted

By now, the contending forces were but six miles from Richmond, which was ringed by a formidable line of fortifications, the fruit of many months' work Grant decided to take the town of Petersburg, lying to the south of Richmond and astride its southbound rail link, the capital's lifeline. Sealing it off, he hoped to starve Richmond into submission, as he had done Vicksburg. But Lee managed to get into position before him, and with 70,000 troops he defended a system of fortifications that extended from the eastern side of Richmond in a sweeping curve to the south of Petersburg. Neither town was to fall into Union hands just yet.

Thus, by the close of June, the Confederates were under severe pressure, their capital on the brink of siege. Yet the people of the North were far from happy with the way things were going. In seven weeks of fighting, the Army of the Potomac had lost 65,000 men. The war had never been less popular. The following month Lee dispatched Jubal Early with a force of 10,000 to raise hell in the Valley, as Jackson had done two years before. In this he succeeded brilliantly, going so far as to approach to the very outskirts of Washington, whose formidable defences his army was far too small to challenge. Panic spread through the Northern capital, and criticism of Lincoln's conduct of the war reached a new degree of severity. Meantime Sherman, after setting out with high expectations, was spending weeks in sparring with rebel troops led by the ever-cautious Johnston. His advance on Atlanta was proceeding at a snail's pace. Though Sherman is known for his brutal remarks, suggestive of a ruthless approach ('War is all hell,' for example), he was in fact chary of involving his men in costly and pointless battles. Both he and Johnston were loath to commit their men to a fight unless they were sure of the outcome. In any case, the need to protect an ever-lengthening line of supply diminished Sherman's advantage in numbers. By mid-summer things looked so bad for Lincoln that he was convinced that were the election to be held in August, he would be bound to lose. Things had not looked so promising for the secessionist cause for many months.

The Shenandoah Valley had long been a source of serious problems to the Federals. In addition to providing a convenient, easily protected route for rebel invasions, it was still providing tons of fodder for Lee's army. Rebel guerrilla units infested its remote valleys, ready to sweep down on helpless Federal supply trains. Grant decided to put a stop to the problem, and he assigned General Phil Sheridan, his chief of cavalry, to do the job. Sheridan hounded the rebels under Early, bringing on a decisive engagement at Cedar Creek in early October. The Confederates fled the Valley, leaving it to the ruthless care of Sheridan, whose army had already spent many weeks in wholesale destruction. Grant had instructed him to turn ' the Shenandoah Valley into a barren waste … so that crows flying over it for the balance of the season will have to carry their provender with them.' Sheridan reported on 7 October that his men had 'destroyed over 2,000 barns filled with wheat, hay and farm implements; over seventy mills filled with flour and wheat; have driven in front of the army over 4,000 head of stock, and have killed and issued to the troops not less than 3,000 sheep.' The devastation of the Valley left an enduring legacy of bitterness among Southerners that lasted for generations.

Sheridan's unparalleled success in the Valley was one reason why Lincoln did not lose the November election. The other was the fall of Atlanta at the beginning of September.

From Atlanta To The Sea

Johnston had persisted in his gradual withdrawal from one well-chosen and heavily fortified position to another, awaiting the moment when Sherman would let his guard slip and expose his army to an annihilating blow – a moment that never came. Despite their high regard for their commanding officer, eventually even his own men began to doubt the wisdom of Johnston's strategy. When, having withdrawn to Atlanta, he seemed on the point of retreating yet again, Davis stepped in and took his army from him. It was time for a bold counterattack, and a former senior officer of Lee's, serving in the west, insisted he could do it. So Davis put John Bell Hood in command. But Hood, though full of fight, was too reckless for so senior a position. He had lost an arm at Gettysburg, and a leg at Chickamauga, and, as a consequence, rode his horse strapped into his saddle. No more aggressive commander ever fought for the South, but, as Lee remarked, he was 'all lion' with 'none of the fox'. When Sherman started to shift his army south around the town, Hood saw an opportunity and smashed into its flank. But hard fighting on both sides led to a stalemate, and the rebels, short of ammunition, pulled back to Atlanta's defences. Continuing his enveloping movement, Sherman cut the rail communications southeast of the town, and forced Hood to pull back. Atlanta had fallen.

Hood now proposed a wildly inappropriate plan: to launch an invasion northwards, liberate Tennessee, and gather recruits along the way. In the vain hope that this might cause Sherman to about face and set off in pursuit, Davis agreed. But the Union commander was not about to oblige, and so there was the strange spectacle of two opposing armies marching off in opposite directions. Sherman detached a force of 60,000 under Thomas to follow and keep an eye on Hood, while, after torching Atlanta, he and the remaining 65,000 began their infamous 'March to the Sea'. Hood's predilection for the attack was to prove his and his army's complete undoing at the battles of Franklin and Nashville, fought with Thomas' men. At the end of December, fragments of his shattered army limped southwards.

Commencing the 285-mile march to Savannah on the Atlantic coast, Sherman declared, 'I shall make Georgia howl.' His army advanced on a front that varied from 25 to 60 miles, burning and pillaging without restraint. Sherman had decided to solve the problem of his line of supply, by living off the land. Despite the acute food shortages that afflicted the Confederacy as a whole, his men found Georgia a relative land of plenty. With no appreciable enemy force ahead of them, his men embarked on what one of them described as 'probably the most gigantic pleasure excursion ever planned'. When they arrived at the state capital, Milledgeville, they made a discovery that added zeal to their wanton destruction. A handful of escaped Union POWs stumbled into camp late one night, so weak they could barely stand, with eyes sunk deep in their sockets, their bones showing so clearly through their flesh that they seemed animated skeletons: they were former inmates of Andersonville.

Andersonville, Pows And Black Soldiers

Set up earlier in the year in the southwest corner of the state, Andersonville was intended as a temporary prison for 10,000. No provisions were made for shelter; the prisoners slept beneath blankets slung along ropes, or in the open air. During a summer of sub-tropical heat, amid primitive sanitation, and with the numbers growing daily, men began to die. By August the camp was home to 33,000 men, and the death rate was a hundred a day. Of the 45,000 held there between the spring and autumn,

13,000 died. After the war, the camp commandant, Henry Wurz, was judicially executed – the only man to be tried for war crimes in the Civil War.

Though undoubtedly responsible, it is unlikely that Wurz in any way intended what happened. The problem of overcrowding, inadequate shelter and malnutrition – a feature of many other Southern prisons – was the result of a number of factors. The shortage of food was the outcome of the blockade imposed by the North, and affected Confederates and their prisoners alike. The ragged and half-starved appearance of the rebel armies was frequently commented on, and Confederate civilians at home fared little better. In the summer of 1864, the women of Richmond led a bread riot, which stopped short of bloodshed only because of Davis's personal intervention. The problem of desertion, which began to sap, the strength of the rebel armies as early as the end of 1863, was created by soldiers wanting to get back home to assist their families in the struggle against hunger. But in addition to this, the population in Southern prisons swelled beyond their capacity because the arrangements for exchanging prisoners, operating earlier in the war, had broken down.

Soldiers taken prisoner at Bull Run or Shiloh were released on an exchange basis. If taken in battle, a soldier could expect to be swapped sooner or later. There was even a scale in operation: a private for a private, an NCO for three privates, an officer for ten and so on. But this exchange process came to a halt over the issue of black troops. Federal units of free blacks and former contrabands were first raised in 1862. Once these began to be used in action, and especially after Lincoln's Emancipation Proclamation, the Confederate government exploded in anger. By recruiting black regiments, the 'Black Republicans' were inciting insurrection, hoping that the slaves in the South would rise up and slaughter their white masters. It refused to treat captured black soldiers as POWs. Whites they would exchange, but the black soldiers, whom they regarded as insurrectionists, they threatened to shoot, or, at the very least, send back into slavery. Lincoln, standing up for the rights of men who had risked their lives to preserve the Union, would not permit a process of exchange that discriminated against black soldiers. It was this that caused the prison numbers in both North and South to grow.

The more barbarous of the threats issued by the South against black soldiers and their white officers were never implemented. There is, however, plenty of evidence of atrocities committed without official sanction by Southern troops against captive black soldiers. It is one of the darker sides of the history of the Confederacy. To cite one example: in April

1864, General Forrest led his cavalry on a raid deep behind Union lines, attacking and destroying Fort Pillow on the Mississippi. It was garrisoned by black troops. Many scores of them were killed while 'attempting to escape' after they had surrendered. In spite of this, by early spring of 1865 the plight of the Confederacy was so desperate that Davis began urging his Congress to legislate for the arming of slaves – a measure that was never put into effect.

The Road To Appomattox

As the year drew to a close, there could be little doubt that the end was in sight. While the South's economy was grinding to a halt, unable to feed and equip the few soldiers still under arms, the North was going from strength to strength. Its blockade of Southern ports was rendered impenetrable by a fleet of nearly 700 warships. Despite losses totalling 300,000, the Union armies currently numbered one million men. 'Material resources,' Lincoln told Congress, 'are now more complete and abundant than ever … we have more men now than we had when the war began…. We are gaining strength and may, if need be, maintain the contest indefinitely.'

For Christmas 1864, Sherman gave Lincoln a present: the city of Savannah. The next leg of his campaign would take his army due north, through the Carolinas, with the objective of coming in on the rear of Lee. The destruction reached a new level of ferocity, for the army was about to enter the heart of secession. Many of Sherman's men regarded South Carolina as responsible for the previous four years, and they resolved to make her pay. The festive atmosphere of the march through Georgia gave way to something altogether grimmer as the challenge of what lay ahead became apparent. They were no longer unopposed, as Johnston, once again back in command, had gathered the remnants of the Confederacy's western forces, and was waiting further north for an opportunity to strike. Furthermore, whereas in summer they had marched 285 miles in fair weather, Sherman's men had now to cover 425 miles of land traversed by impassable swamps and countless creeks, in the depths of one of the wettest winters on record. But Northern engineering ingenuity – laying miles of improvised road across raw swamp – coupled with an unshakeable resolve to finish the campaign, enabled Sherman to push his army far into North Carolina.

Through the winter, Lee's army held on outside Richmond and Petersburg. Grant's repeated probing towards the south had caused the line of trenches to extend 35 miles; Lee's army, wasting away from desertion, was stretched to breaking point. At the end of March, the climax began when, in a bold move, Lee went on the attack and, against all the odds, seized Fort Steadman at the centre of Grant's line. But they could not hold on to it. Driving the rebels back to their lines, Grant replied by sending a force under Sheridan round Lee's right flank. Pickett's division tried to repel the Federal troops, but it collapsed in the attempt. With his line flanked, Lee decided to abandon the Petersburg trenches. Three years and eight months after they first set out to capture it, Union troops entered Richmond.

Lee and what was left of his army hurried southwest, just ahead of the pursuing Federals, hoping to join Johnston and inflict a defeat on Sherman before Grant was on top of them. The fighting continued. On 8 April, the rebels were surrounded – 33,000 facing an army of 120,000. Rejecting the suggestion that his army scatter, and continue the war as partisans, Lee sued for terms. Next day at Appomattox Courthouse, Grant accepted his surrender.

A week later, Johnston capitulated to Sherman. Jeff Davis was apprehended en route to the west, where he hoped to join the last rebel armies still holding out across the Mississippi. Without a government, or a credible armed force, the Confederacy was at an end.

Postlude: A War For Freedom?

What did the death of 620,000 Americans achieve?

Freedom

In the pre-war years, the ordinary citizen would have encountered central government chiefly through its control of the national postal system. In most other areas of his or her life, it was possible to evade it, so restricted was the scope of its power. But the war transformed this state of affairs. Central government had imposed direct, albeit limited, taxation, and a bureau of internal revenue to administer it; the jurisdiction of federal courts had mushroomed; a national currency and federally chartered banking system had been established; men had been drafted into the army, though in limited numbers; and the first agency of social welfare, the Freedmen's Bureau, to administer the needs of the newly liberated blacks, had been set up. Not only did these functions represent a terrific increase in the power of central government, they also set a precedent for still further growth. The balance of power between Washington and the state capitals was tilted firmly towards the former. Eleven of the first twelve Amendments to the Constitution had been framed to restrain the power of central government – all adopted before the war. Of the Amendments that followed the war, six of the first seven expanded the powers of central government at the expense of the states.

The Confederacy had gone to war expressly to resist the burgeoning of central government at the expense of the states, to resist the 'tyranny' of Lincoln's Republican administration. Anticipating an attack on their cherished 'peculiar institution', they had launched a war that had brought about that very growth of Federal power they feared. There is no reason to believe that Lincoln intended any radical programme to transfer power in this way. It was an unforeseen consequence of the need to win the war.

From the point of view of the freedom of the individual, does this represent a gain or a loss? At the start I considered two notions of freedom: 'negative freedom', the being let alone to pursue one's chosen path to happiness; and 'positive freedom', in which one's need to be equipped with a range of basic life-provisions, from housing and health to education, in order to flourish, for freedom to have positive value, was recognised. The former takes for granted that the basic means to lead a fruitful life are already in place, and are not the responsibility of government to provide. The one represents the Southern, the other the Northern view.

With the growth of central government, individuals would be increasingly liable to regulation and control by a power remote from their locality. The war represents, then, a defeat for the freedom simply to be let alone, for the beneficiaries of inherited wealth or those who prefer to live on the margins of society: but a victory for those, like the immigrants from Europe and the newly emancipated blacks, who needed government to provide the necessary conditions for the pursuit of happiness.

The full working out of the role of central government as an agent of social welfare was to take much of the ensuing century, but the seeds were sown with the Civil War.

Equality

Four million slaves were freed by the war. The Thirteenth Amendment to the Constitution shut the door on the 'peculiar institution' for good. But in the immediate post-war period a struggle ensued between the needs of reconciliation between North and South, on the one hand, and the ascription of equal status to the blacks, on the other. For equality, two further things beside emancipation were needed: the guarantee of basic rights, including the right to vote and hold office; and the provision of land to curtail economic dependence.

During the course of the war, Lincoln travelled a long way to acknowledging the need to include the blacks in the political process. Key here was the role played by some 170,000 black soldiers in the defence of the Union. Others in the North had been similarly impressed. But the conservative majority in the North – outside New England, no free blacks could vote – would not have rushed into universal black suffrage had it not been for the intransigence of the post-war South. Lincoln's death brought to office his vice-president. A former slave-owner from Tennessee, Andrew Johnson, was a racist eager to curry favour with Southern leaders. On the condition that they submit to the authority of the Federal government and its antislavery measures, and renounced the right of secession, he permitted Southerners to ratify state constitutions, and to hold state and Federal elections. Eight months after the war, an unrepentant Southern elite had once again resumed its seat in Congress. Worse still, Southern states began trying to reintroduce a variation on the 'peculiar institution'; codes were adopted regulating the rights of free blacks to a degree little short of their former condition as slaves.

This provoked a radical reaction in the North. Moderates rallied behind the extreme platform that advocated full rights for the blacks.

Scores of thousands of the former Confederate elite were disenfranchised and debarred from holding office. The Southern states were ejected from the Union and divided between five military districts, only permitted back once they had new constitutions that incorporated black suffrage. Southern whites feared complete subordination to their former slaves, for, with a considerable number of them having been disenfranchised, they were a minority of the electorate.

But in a few years, South's white elite was once again in control. How did this come about? The chief reason was their economic power. Attempts to establish the freed blacks as an independent yeomanry fell foul of the North's readiness to be reconciled with its former enemy. A general amnesty was the order of the day, and land that had been confiscated was usually handed back to its former owners, even if this meant displacing former slaves who had been settled on it by the invading Union armies. Deprived of control over the means of earning a living, the blacks were forced into dependence on white landowners. Working as farm labourers, or as tenants under the sharecropping system, blacks were at the mercy of their white bosses, who dictated how they would vote. By the mid-1870s, black representation in the legislatures of the Southern states was waning. Segregation of schools, healthcare and housing became firmly entrenched, and the black was relegated to the status of second-class citizen – a status not to be challenged for a hundred years.

Chronology

1776

Declaration of Independence

1793

Eli Whitney invents the 'Cotton Gin'

1803

Louisiana Purchase

1807

Slave trade outlawed for British merchant ships

1820

Missouri Compromise

1822

Slave insurrection led by Denmark Vesey

1831

Abolitionist newspaper *The Liberator* founded by William Lloyd Garrison

1832

Slave insurrection led by Nat Turner

1846-48

War with Mexico

1850

Settlement of problems arising from acquisition of Mexican territory, known as the '1850 Compromise'

1851

Harriet Beecher Stowe publishes *Uncle Tom's Cabin*

1854

Kansas applies for admission to the Union

1856

Fighting in Kansas between 'slave' and 'free' factions

1857

Dred Scott Case

1859

John Brown seizes Federal arsenal at Harper's Ferry
November, Lincoln elected

December, South Carolina secedes from the Union

1861

February, Jefferson Davis elected president of the Confederacy
12 April, Fort Sumter fired upon
19 April, Lincoln proclaims blockade of Southern ports
21 July, First Battle of Bull Run (eastern theatre of war)
November, Southern envoys Mason and Slidell arrested while en route to Europe

1862

February, Grant captures forts Henry and Donelson (western theatre)
6 April, Battle of Shiloh (western theatre)
26 April, Federals capture New Orleans (western theatre)
April-June, McClellan's Peninsula Campaign (eastern theatre)
May-June, Jackson's campaign in the Shenandoah Valley (eastern theatre)
August-October, Bragg's invasion of Kentucky (western theatre)
29 August, Battle of Manassas (eastern theatre)
17 September, Battle of Antietam (eastern theatre)
22 September, Lincoln issues Emancipation Proclamation
October, Grant launches campaign against Vicksburg (western theatre)
7 October, Battle of Perryville (western theatre)
13 December, Battle of Fredericksburg (eastern theatre)

1863

1-3 January, Battle of Stones River (western theatre)
30 April to 3 May, Battle of Chancellorsville (eastern theatre)
1-3 July, Battle of Gettysburg (eastern theatre)
4 July, Grant captures Vicksburg
20 September, Battle of Chickamauga (western theatre)
24-25 November, Battle of Chattanooga (western theatre)

1864

March, Grant appointed supreme commander of Union armies
May, Sherman begins campaign to take Atlanta (western theatre)
5 May to 3 June, from 'the Wilderness' to Cold Harbour (eastern theatre)
June, siege of Richmond and Petersburg begins (eastern theatre)
July, Jubal Early's campaign in the Shenandoah Valley
August to October, Sheridan's Valley campaign

1 September, Sherman captures Atlanta
15 November, 'March to the Sea' begins
21 December, Sherman captures Savannah, begins march north
through the Carolinas

1865

March, 13th Amendment to the Constitution banning slavery
3 April, Lee abandons defence of Richmond and Petersburg
9 April, Lee surrenders to Grant at Appomattox Courthouse
14 April, John Wilkes Booth assassinates Lincoln
26 April, Johnston surrenders to Sherman

Recommended Reading

Battle Cry of Freedom: the American Civil War James McPherson
(Penguin)

Conflict and Transformation: The United States 1844-1877 William R
Brock (Penguin)

Personal Memoirs Ulysses S Grant (Penguin)

Battles and Leaders of the Civil War 4 vols, articles by participants in the
war (Thomas Yoseloff)

Drawn with the Sword: Reflections on the American Civil War James
McPherson (Oxford University Press)

History of the Army of the Potomac by Bruce Catton
  Mr Lincoln's Army (Scribner)
  Glory Road (Scribner)
  A Stillness at Appomattox (Scribner)

The Essential Library

Build up your library with new titles every month

Conspiracy Theories by Robin Ramsay, £3.99

Do you think the X-Files is fiction? That Elvis is dead? That the US actually went to the moon? And don't know that the ruling elite did a deal with the extra-terrestrials after the Roswell crash in 1947... At one time, you could blame the world's troubles on the Masons or the Illuminati, or the Jews, or One Worlders, or the Great Communist Conspiracy. Now we also have the alien-US elite conspiracy, or the alien shape-shifting reptile conspiracy to worry about - and there are books to prove it as well! This book tries to sort out the handful of wheat from the choking clouds of intellectual chaff. For among the nonsensical Conspiracy Theory rubbish currently proliferating on the Internet, there are important nuggets of real research about real conspiracies waiting to be mined.

Alchemy & Alchemists by Sean Martin, £3.99

Alchemy is often seen as an example of medieval gullibility and the alchemists as a collection of eccentrics and superstitious fools. Sean Martin shows that nothing could be further from the truth. It is important to see the search for the philosopher's stone and the attempts to turn base metal into gold as metaphors for the relation of man to nature and man to God as much as seriously held beliefs. Alchemists like Paracelsus and Albertus Magnus were amongst the greatest minds of their time. This book traces the history of alchemy from ancient times to the 20th century, highlighting the interest of modern thinkers like Jung in the subject. It covers a major, if neglected area of Western thought.

Black Death by Sean Martin, £3.99

The Black Death is the name most commonly given to the pandemic of bubonic plague that ravaged the medieval world in the late 1340s. From Central Asia the plague swept through Europe, leaving millions of dead in its wake. Between a quarter and a third of Europe's population died. In England the population fell from nearly six million to just over three million. The Black Death was the greatest demographic disaster in European history.

The Crusades by Mike Paine, £3.99

The first crusade was set in motion by Pope Urban II in 1095 and culminated in the capture of Jerusalem from the Muslims four years later. In 1291 the fall of Acre marked the loss of the last Christian enclave in the Holy Land. This Pocket Essential traces the chronology of the Crusades between these two dates and highlights the most important figures on all sides of the conflict.

Ancient Greece by Mike Paine, £3.99 (Published 2002)

Western civilization began with the Greeks. From the highpoint of the 5th century BC through the cultural triumphs of the Alexandrian era to their impact on the developing Roman empire, the Greeks shaped the philosophy, art, architecture and literature of the Mediterranean world. Mike Paine provides a concise and well-informed narrative of many centuries of Greek history. He highlights the careers of great political and military leaders like Pericles and Alexander the Great, and shows the importance of the great philosophers like Plato and Aristotle. Dramatists and demagogues, stoics and epicureans, aristocrats and helots take their places in the unfolding story of the Greek achievement.

The Essential Library

Build up your library with new titles every month

Film Directors:

Jane Campion (£2.99)   **John Carpenter** (£3.99)
Jackie Chan (£2.99)   **Joel & Ethan Coen** (£3.99)
David Cronenberg (£3.99)   **Terry Gilliam** (£2.99)
Alfred Hitchcock (£3.99)   **Krzysztof Kieslowski** (£2.99)
Stanley Kubrick (£2.99)   **Sergio Leone** (£3.99)
David Lynch (£3.99)   **Brian De Palma** (£2.99)
Sam Peckinpah (£2.99)   **Ridley Scott** (£3.99)
Orson Welles (£2.99)   **Billy Wilder** (£3.99)
Steven Spielberg (£3.99)

Film Genres:

Film Noir (£3.99)   **Hong Kong Heroic Bloodshed** (£2.99)
Horror Films (£3.99)   **Slasher Movies**(£3.99)
Spaghetti Westerns (£3.99) **Vampire Films** (£2.99)
Blaxploitation Films (£3.99)

Film Subjects:

Laurel & Hardy (£3.99)   **Marx Brothers** (£3.99)
Steve McQueen (£2.99)   **Marilyn Monroe** (£3.99)
The Oscars® (£3.99)   **Filming On A Microbudget** (£3.99)
Bruce Lee (£3.99)

TV:

Doctor Who (£3.99)

Literature:

Cyberpunk (£3.99)   **Philip K Dick** (£3.99)
Hitchhiker's Guide (£3.99) **Noir Fiction** (£2.99)
Terry Pratchett (£3.99)   **Sherlock Holmes** (£3.99)

Ideas:

Conspiracy Theories (£3.99) **Nietzsche** (£3.99)
Feminism (£3.99)

History:

Alchemy & Alchemists (£3.99)   **The Crusades** (£3.99)

Available at all good bookstores, or send a cheque to: **Pocket Essentials (Dept CW), 18 Coleswood Rd, Harpenden, Herts, AL5 1EQ, UK**. Please make cheques payable to 'Oldcastle Books.' Add 50p postage & packing for each book in the UK and £1 elsewhere.

US customers can send $6.95 plus $1.95 postage & packing for each book to: **Trafalgar Square Publishing, PO Box 257, Howe Hill Road, North Pomfret, Vermont 05053, USA**. e-mail: tsquare@sover.net

Customers worldwide can order online at **www.pocketessentials.com**.

The Essential Library

Build up your library with new titles every month

Tim Burton by Colin Odell & Michelle Le Blanc, £3.99

Tim Burton makes films about outsiders on the periphery of society. His heroes are psychologically scarred, perpetually naive and childlike, misunderstood or unintentionally disruptive. They upset convential society and morality. Even his villains are rarely without merit - circumstance blurs the divide between moral fortitude and personal action. But most of all, his films have an aura of the fairytale, the fantastical and the magical.

Film Music by Paul Tonks, £3.99

From *Ben-Hur* to *Star Wars* and *Psycho* to *Scream*, film music has played an essential role in such genre-defining classics. Making us laugh, cry, and jump with fright, it's the manipulative tool directors cannot do without. The turbulent history, the ever-changing craft, the reclusive or limelight-loving superstars, the enthusiastic world of fandom surrounding it, and the best way to build a collection, is all streamlined into a user-friendly guide for buffs and novices alike.

Woody Allen (Revised & Updated Edition) by Martin Fitzgerald, £3.99

Woody Allen: Neurotic. Jewish. Funny. Inept. Loser. A man with problems. Or so you would think from the characters he plays in his movies. But hold on. Allen has written and directed 30 films. He may be a funny man, but he is also one of the most serious American film-makers of his generation. This revised and updated edition includes *Sweet And Lowdown* and *Small Time Crooks*.

American Civil War by Phil Davies, £3.99

The American Civil War, fought between North and South in the years 1861-1865, was the bloodiest and most traumatic war in American history. Rival visions of the future of the United States faced one another across the battlefields and, as in any civil war, families and friends were bitterly divided by the conflict. Phil Davies looks at the deep-rooted causes of the war, so much more complicated than the simple issue of slavery.

American Indian Wars by Howard Hughes, £3.99

At the beginning of the 1840s the proud tribes of the North American Indians looked across the plains at the seemingly unstoppable expansion of the white man's West. During the decades of conflict that followed, as the new world pushed onward, the Indians saw their way of life disappear before their eyes. Over the next 40 years they clung to a dream of freedom and a continuation of their traditions, a dream that was repeatedly shattered by the whites.

Available at all good bookstores, or send a cheque to: **Pocket Essentials (Dept CW), 18 Coleswood Rd, Harpenden, Herts, AL5 1EQ, UK**. Please make cheques payable to 'Oldcastle Books.' Add 50p postage & packing for each book in the UK and £1 elsewhere.

US customers can send $6.95 plus $1.95 postage & packing for each book to: **Trafalgar Square Publishing, PO Box 257, Howe Hill Road, North Pomfret, Vermont 05053, USA**. e-mail: tsquare@sover.net

Customers worldwide can order online at **www.pocketessentials.com**.